# OREGON
# SPORTS STORIES

## HISTORY, HIGHLIGHTS & REFLECTIONS

# OREGON SPORTS STORIES

## HISTORY, HIGHLIGHTS & REFLECTIONS

BOB ROBINSON

THE History PRESS

Published by The History Press
Charleston, SC 29403
www.historypress.net



First published 2013

Manufactured in the United States

ISBN 978.1.62619.157.0

Library of Congress CIP data applied for.

*Notice*: The information in this book is true and complete to the best of our knowledge. It is offered without guarantee on the part of the author or The History Press. The author and The History Press disclaim all liability in connection with the use of this book.

# Contents

# Preface

I was eight years old in the fall of 1942 when I attended my first college football game. Excited? An understatement. I was in major awe of the atmosphere at Bell Field on the Oregon State campus. The school in Corvallis was called Oregon State College in those days, with a name change to Oregon State University to come later.

My father, Paul Robinson, took me to the game from our home in the small Willamette Valley town of Independence, best known for its hop-growing industry. The Beavers were playing their home opener against California. The attendance was estimated at 11,500, small by current standards but seemingly huge to me at the time.

This was the season after Oregon State's improbable 20–16 upset of Duke in the Rose Bowl game that was transplanted to Durham, North Carolina, because of the World War II threat of Japanese bombing on the West Coast. I already was kind of a sports nut, and I had followed the bowl team's games via newspapers and the radio. Now I was seeing the real thing, and I was thrilled.

As luck would have it, the game was a dramatic one. I stood and cheered right along with my father as the Beavers, trailing 8–6 late in the game, put together a last-ditch drive for a potential winning touchdown or field goal. I still have reasonably vivid recollections of that scene so long ago.

The game clock had moved inside the final minute as the Beavers got to within a yard of the goal at the far end of the field from our seats. Spectators were jumping up and down and waving their arms. I remember my father's laughter when he noticed that I had my fingers crossed on both hands. Then the ball was handed off to Everett Smith, who drove off tackle and into the end zone with ten seconds remaining. Moments later, the celebration was on over Oregon State's 13–8 victory.

"Maybe they'll go to the Rose Bowl again," I said to my father, who had attended Oregon State and was a varsity swimmer when the school was called Oregon Agricultural College, with the nickname of Aggies. He smiled and replied, "It's a little early to think about that."

It turned out that he was correct. The Beavers had to settle for a record of four wins, five losses and a tie.

Still, that 1942 game became a factor in drawing me toward a sportswriting career, thirty-seven and a half years of it at the *Oregonian*. It was something like *The Wizard of Oz* movie, starring the late Judy Garland. I seemed to have been pointed down my own version of the yellow brick road.

I covered many exciting games and other events spanning six decades. I met so many interesting personalities. Sharing my memories of some of these experiences and personalities is what this book is about. The project also pushed me to call on storytelling skills—an enjoyable experience.

# Acknowledgements

Many people earned my gratitude for helping with this project. Among them were sports media representatives Steve Fenk of Oregon State University, Greg Walker of the University of Oregon and Mike Lund of Portland State University who tracked down many of the picture images that appear in the book. I also give thanks to *Oregonian* photographers Brent Wojahn and Thomas Boyd for the use of their photos. Drew Vattiat of the *Oregonian* deserves kudos, too, for patiently digging through the newspaper's archives to find me photos from long ago. Roger Jensen, Rob Griffin, Tom Treick and Mike Shields were other contributing photographers.

The Portland Trail Blazers, through retired historian Chuck Charnquist, helped immensely by providing photos from the club's archives. I also offer thanks to the National Greyhound Racing Association for its help, to Mac Wilkins who provided photos from his personal collection and to Wayne Thompson and Nick Bertram for some editing suggestions. In addition, Aubrie Koenig, my commissioning editor, was top notch with her encouragement.

Lastly, I express special appreciation to my daughter, Nan Hammerschmidt, for her line drawing and to my grandson, Jean-Paul Wallis, who used his computer savvy to help me survive the challenge of formatting and delivering the manuscript.

# 1

# How Could You, Mr. McKay?

It seemed a little weird, but there was John McKay, a University of Oregon assistant football coach, ready to instruct a basketball class at the Eugene school. It was 1954 and an era when many assistant coaches fulfilled teaching duties in physical education departments.

I happened to be in that class, and I already was acquainted with McKay from his friendship with my cousin Darrell Robinson. I first was introduced to him at the Eugene home of Darrell's parents in 1947, when the two UO football teammates happened to drop by for a visit.

Anyway, that was long before McKay would move on to a Hall of Fame coaching career at the University of Southern California. He obviously wasn't particularly happy to be in charge of that PE class, and in the second week, he called me aside.

"Rob, I want you to do something for me," he said. "I'm not going to be here for class at times, and I want you to be in charge when I'm not here. Divide the guys into teams and have a tournament, or whatever you think is appropriate. I know you will handle it."

He then handed me a key to the closet where the basketballs were stored. And starting with the next class session, it was my class for all intents and purposes, beginning with the fetching of balls from the closet. John stopped by regularly to see how things were going but seldom stayed for long.

McKay asked me at the end of the term if there had been any "bad actors" in the class. I told him there weren't any. In fact, I'd enjoyed the experience. I didn't get much static from other members of the class. They

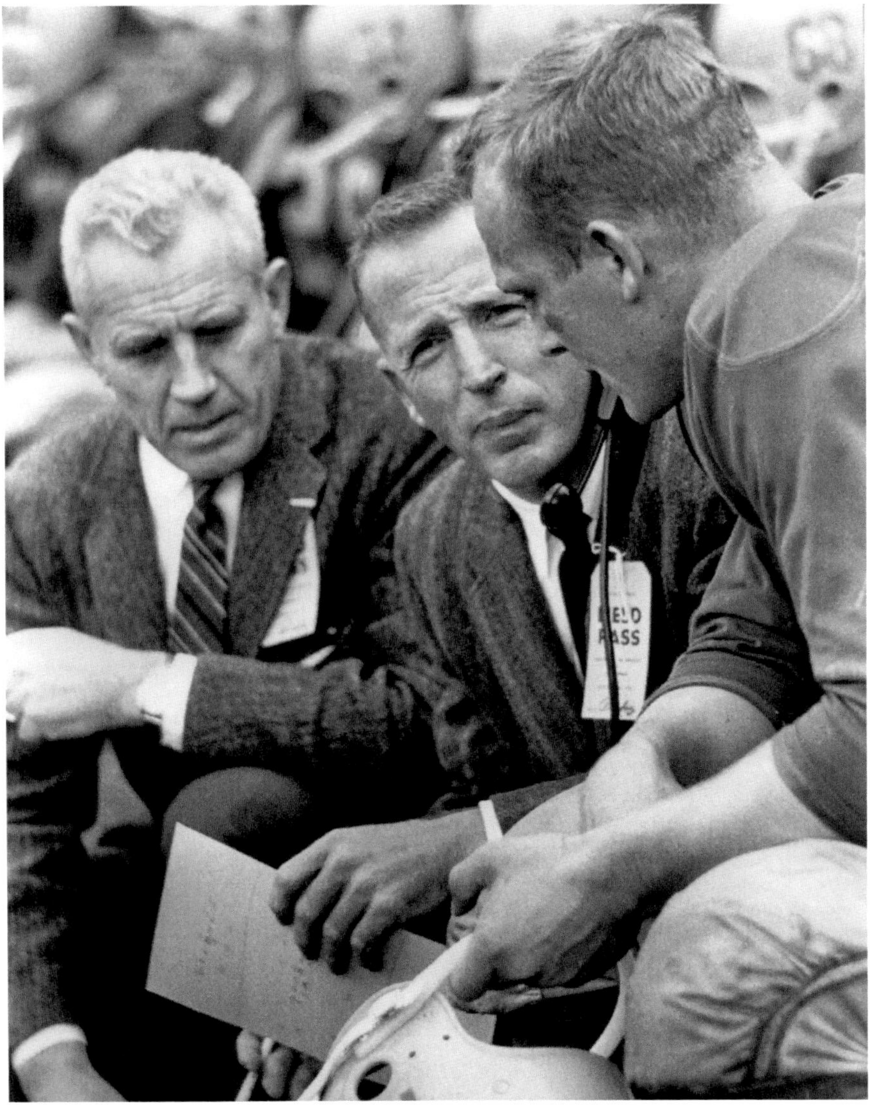


John McKay (middle), then an Oregon assistant, talks strategy with Ducks coach Len Casanova (left) and quarterback Jack Crabtree in 1957. *Courtesy of UO Athletics Media Relations.*

seemed perfectly content participating in the scrimmage games and other contests that I organized.

About a week after the term ended, I got my grades. I was flabbergasted. McKay had given me a B. My first inclination was to go to him in protest. Finally, though, I could laugh about my bizarre situation. It was only one hour of credit, and I wasn't about to give him the satisfaction of thinking I was upset.

Two weeks later, as a sportswriter for the *Daily Emerald*, the school newspaper, I was on my way to do an interview with track and field coach Bill Bowerman at his office in McArthur Court. As I walked down the hall, I saw McKay talking to a couple of fellow coaches. He happened to look over his shoulder and saw me approaching. He turned to face me.

"Now, Rob, I want you to understand something," he said. "I didn't give anyone an A in that class."

Before he could say anything else, I said, "I'm not here to see you, John. I'm just on my way to Bowerman's office." And I kept right on walking. That was that—or so I thought.

McKay, who had a career average of more than six yards per carry for the 1947–49 UO teams as a running back, was a standout on the 1948 team that featured Norm Van Brocklin at quarterback and earned a berth in the 1949 Cotton Bowl, where the Ducks lost to Southern Methodist 21–13.

"John was an unusual person, kind of unpredictable," said teammate Robinson, who was best man at McKay's wedding. "He was very intelligent, and he had a great memory. I think he remembered every joke that he ever heard."

Keep that comment in mind as you read on to the end of this essay.

On the football field, Robinson said McKay was like having a coach in the huddle. Under coach Jim Aiken, he often was asked to call plays.

"He was one of those guys who knew what every player was supposed to do on every play," said Robinson, an end for the Ducks and one of Van Brocklin's favorite receivers. "When John spoke, you listened. He always seemed to be two steps ahead of everyone else."

I saw several of the 1948 team's games, including a 10–0 win over Oregon State at muddy Bell Field in Corvallis. McKay scored the Ducks' touchdown on a seventeen-yard end sweep.

As years passed and I progressed in my sportswriting career, I saw McKay occasionally as I worked at games involving his Trojans, who claimed national championships in 1962, 1967, 1972 and 1974. One of those times was in 1967, when USC was upset by Oregon State's aptly nicknamed Giant Killers 3–0 in Corvallis on another muddy field.

McKay, who was seventy-seven when he died in 2001, did a masterful job of bringing that team, featuring running back O.J. Simpson, back to earn the national title despite its loss to the Beavers.

I also enjoyed reading about some of the one-liners that made him a writer's dream.

John McKay, here at a team practice, gained most of his fame while coaching Southern California to four national championships. *Courtesy of USC Athletics Media Relations.*

Following a 51–0 loss to Notre Dame in 1966, he said, "I told my team it didn't matter. There are 750 million people in China who don't even know this game was played."

After a game in 1967, he was asked why Simpson carried the ball so much. "Why not?" he replied. "The ball is not heavy, and he doesn't belong to a union."

What happened before the Trojans' game at Notre Dame in 1967 was another McKay gem. He knew how the Irish coaches liked to have the visiting team come onto the field first just before the kickoff, hoping to intimidate the visitors with the bedlam of Notre Dame's rollicking entrance. So McKay decided to keep his team inside until the Irish were already on the field.

About ten minutes before the scheduled kickoff, a Notre Dame representative came to the locker room to tell McKay that it was time for his team to go onto the field. John said he would wait until the Irish were on the field. Twice more, the representative came calling, with the same reaction from McKay. On the third trip, the representative told McKay that if his team didn't go onto the field immediately, a forfeit might be declared.

"That's fine," McKay said. "A forfeit is 2–0; that's a lot better than our 51–0 loss last year."

Finally, the Irish preceded USC onto the field. Then the Trojans rolled to a 24–7 win, with Simpson running for 160 yards.

Later, when McKay was coaching Tampa Bay of the National Football League and the Bucs were struggling to end a losing streak, he was asked what he thought of his team's execution. "I'm all for it," he said.

Now fast-forward to 1980, when I was covering Oregon State's football team for the *Oregonian*. The Beavers had lost at Arizona State on a Saturday night and then took a flight early Sunday to Dallas, where they would practice for five days before going to Austin to play Texas the following Saturday.

I was assigned to spend the week covering the Beavers in their preparations for the Longhorns. So I was in Dallas, too, on that Sunday when the Cowboys were scheduled to play host to McKay's Bucs. I arranged to have a seat in the press box. I was planning to just watch the game, not write about it.

That plan changed when Tom Blanchard, a former University of Oregon quarterback and punter, had a sensational punting performance for Tampa Bay. His kicking kept the underdog Bucs in the game until the final minutes before the Cowboys prevailed 28–17.

I decided to do a story on Blanchard and went to the Tampa Bay locker room. After interviewing him, I asked an assistant coach where McKay was hanging out. He pointed out a room with the door closed and said to just go ahead and enter.

I opened the door, and there was McKay, slumped on a bench at the far end of the room. He looked up at me, and I swear, the first thing he said was, "You're still upset about that B, aren't you?"

I laughed, shook his hand and said, "John, if you still remember that, you must have a guilty conscience."

He grinned and said, "You think? Well, maybe so."

# 2
# A Mouse with a Vision

Ask Mouse Davis when he first started to develop his Run and Shoot football offense and he'll talk about his early years as a high school coach. But when I suggested to him that it might go back even further—to when he was a quarterback at Independence High School in Oregon's Willamette Valley in 1947–49—he grinned and said, "I guess that's possible."

When Davis was a senior, I was a sophomore end for the uniquely named Hopsters, and I remember how he frequently added his own wrinkles to the team's playbook. More than once, Davis came off the field to be greeted by a "What was that?" from coach John Mathis or one of his assistants.

In an early season game against Dayton, we were ahead 31–0 in the fourth quarter. It was garbage time, and a bunch of us younger players were sent into the game. Davis, though, remained on the field to keep the offense from turning into chaos.

We were on the Dayton thirty-yard line. Davis immediately called a timeout and pulled me aside from the huddle. "Look, I'm going to get you a touchdown," he said. "They just sent in a new defensive back on your side. We're going to run the fake pitchout play. Split out a couple of yards farther than normal and delay two seconds after the snap. Then run right at that back and cut to the sideline. And don't you dare drop the ball."

Already nervous, I suddenly bordered on panic. The play unfolded, and I silently counted off the two seconds and took off. I made my cut, and the defensive back didn't go with me. I was wide open. I turned and saw that Davis's pass already was on the way. I felt my nerves tingling, but I managed

Mouse Davis, getting ready for action, was offensive coordinator on his second tour of duty at Portland State. *Courtesy of PSU Athletics Media Relations.*

to catch it and run into the end zone. Needless to say, I was excited about scoring my first high school touchdown. But I think that Mouse was even more excited.

Even though I was two school classes behind him, Davis and I had become good friends. I had one of the few backyard basketball hoops in the small town, undoubtedly a factor in that friendship. So, too, might have been the fact that I could get the keys to the high school gym on weekends from my father, Paul Robinson, the high school principal.

Davis threw three more scoring passes to me that season. One of them also involved creative variations from the playbook. After that game, Mouse came up to me, and he was chuckling. "Let's see what you write about that one," he said.

That wasn't a major problem for me as I wrote stories on the games for the weekly *Independence Enterprise*. Mouse got mentioned, and so did his receiver.

The point is that Davis already was becoming innovative and creative in his thinking about football. And in the 1950 *Cardinal*, the high school yearbook, he listed "Be a coach" in the ambition line under his senior picture.

Mouse Davis has to look up to give instructions to a player before a Portland State game in the late 1970s. *Courtesy of PSU Athletics Media Relations.*

Davis once said of his five-foot-six height, "I got that tall, then went into a holding pattern."

His older brother, Don, was responsible for his nickname. Until he was fourteen, he was simply Darrel Davis.

"It was during a baseball workout," he said. "All of a sudden, Don yelled out 'Mouse' at me, and I have been stuck with the name ever since. It bothered me for a while, but long ago I became cool with it."

His size never kept Davis idle in high school sports. In addition to football, he played basketball (as a playmaking guard) and baseball (as a second baseman). He even took up distance running for the track team in his senior year. Then he went on to Oregon College of Education (now Western Oregon University), where he played football under legendary coach Bill McArthur and also was on the basketball and baseball teams.

Davis also endeared himself to many of his fellow high school students when, as a senior, he was responsible for getting boxing removed from the school's physical education program. He did it by knocking out his opponent, who had made some derogatory comments about him behind his back. The

KO brought instant backlash from some teachers and parents, and boxing in PE classes quickly became history.

Davis's Run and Shoot—with as many as five wide receivers and no tight end—started taking root at Milwaukie High School, his second head-coaching job. He already had installed much of the offense before he got around to reading a book by Glenn "Tiger" Ellison, recognized as the creator of the Run and Shoot.

"What I got from Ellison's book was the idea to use a double-slotback formation," he said. "I hadn't been using that before."

The rest, you might say, is history, and I had occasions over the years to write stories about Davis for the *Oregonian*. I covered the game at the University of Oregon's Autzen Stadium in 1973, when his Hillsboro Spartans claimed the big-school state championship.

Asked by a reporter about his nickname after that game, he jokingly replied, "I wouldn't want to be called Darrel now. Folks might forget that I coached these guys."

From the outset, Davis constantly heard skeptics say that his offense might be OK at the high school level but that it wouldn't work at the game's higher levels. If Davis had any doubts, he never showed them.

He became head coach at Portland State in 1975, and his teams, over six seasons, set all kinds of NCAA passing, scoring and total offense records. The Vikings went 42-24 through the 1980 season, and home attendance climbed spectacularly. The skeptics had to admit that the Run and Shoot could work at the college level, too.

In 1975, when PSU still was in NCAA Division II, quarterback June Jones passed for a division record of 3,518 yards. While becoming the first college quarterback to excel in the Run and Shoot, he passed for 5,798 yards and fifty touchdowns in his two seasons at PSU.

June Jones was Mouse Davis's first outstanding quarterback in his Run and Shoot offense at Portland State. *Courtesy of PSU Athletics Media Relations.*

After Jones, there was Neil Lomax, who virtually rewrote the record book for NCAA Division I-A. In 1977–80, the lightly recruited Lomax passed for 13,220 yards and 106 touchdowns in forty-two games. As a senior, he passed for 4,094 yards in eleven games.

"Not bad for a kid who had trouble getting a college scholarship," Davis said.

Lomax earned All-America honors and later was selected for the College Football Hall of Fame. Both Jones and Lomax played in the NFL, and Jones had Davis as an assistant while he was head coach of the Atlanta Falcons. Davis loved to talk about Lomax, going back to the days when he recruited him out of Oregon's Lake Oswego High School.

"He played under Boyd Long at Lake Oswego, and Boyd didn't have his teams pass much," Davis said. "So Neil wasn't getting much attention (as a college prospect) because he was only throwing the ball seven or eight times a game, mostly short routes."

Davis remembers well the last time he went to one of Lomax's high school games.

"I stayed for the warm-ups to see him pass the ball," Davis told me. "Then I left before the game started. I had seen all I needed to see."

By the time Lomax was a PSU senior, he was piling up numbers that were off the charts. He even threw a national-record seven touchdown passes in the first quarter against Delaware State! The Vikings, with all except the team manager seeing action, wound up with a 105–0 victory.

A series of Delaware State turnovers and first-play scoring passes by Lomax led to the amazing first quarter.

"He already had passed for six TDs and, even with a bunch of subs in on defense, we got the ball back with a minute left in the quarter," Davis recalled. "I asked Neil what he wanted to do. He said, 'Let's go for it.' Darned if he didn't go out and pass for that seventh score (before the end of the quarter)."

Anyway, those Portland State teams got Davis the recognition he needed to earn a shot at coaching the pro game. His resume looked like alphabet soup, as he had stops in the USFL (U.S. Football League), the WLAB (World League of American Football), the AFL (Arena Football League), the CFL (Canadian Football League) and, finally, the NFL. To say that Davis was well traveled would be a gross understatement.

There were ups and downs along the way. But the Run and Shoot seldom failed to be exciting. There were times—when Davis was an assistant with the Detroit Lions and had Barry Sanders as a running back and then with the Falcons—that the offense appeared ready to really take off. At Atlanta,

Neil Lomax, lightly recruited out of high school, fires a pass on his way to a record-breaking career at Portland State. *Courtesy of PSU Athletics Media Relations.*

he had a head coach in Jones who naturally was an all-in advocate of the Run and Shoot.

But Jones and Davis, partially because of injuries to key players, didn't get over the hump with the Falcons, and Jones eventually returned to college coaching at the University of Hawaii, where he hired Davis as an assistant to help refine the offense. Later, Jones moved on to Southern Methodist University, and Davis spent time as an assistant to Jerry Glanville at Portland State, where the team's offense was productive but the defense was a disaster.

Then, after a retirement that turned out to be temporary, Davis took what he figured would be "one last fling" in coaching—a two-year stint as an assistant to Greg McMacken at Hawaii for the 2010 and 2011 seasons. Then, at seventy-nine, he settled into a less stressful life with his wife, Mary Lou, at their home in Lake Oswego.

"I didn't have to do it, but I just loved coaching," he said of his final two years in Hawaii with McMacken.

In retirement, he became an analyst for Portland State football telecasts and improved his golf game enough to shoot better than his age, with a seventy-six at Portland's Glendoveer course.

Through the years, Davis observed major changes in offensive schemes of coaches at all levels. Virtually all of them turned to using multiple wide outs with the quarterback, often operating out of the shotgun, getting reads off the defense and reacting. Principles of the Run and Shoot could be seen everywhere, especially in the spread offenses that became so popular.

"I still get a lot of calls from coaches asking me for thoughts on their philosophies," Davis said shortly before his final retirement. "I can't help but feel good about whatever impact I have had."

In 2012, Davis was inducted into the Oregon Sports Hall of Fame. But long before that, it had dawned on me that my friend with the unusual nickname was a football guru.

# 3

# It All Began with Dellinger

Bill Dellinger always seemed to be a quiet one in the days when we were classmates at the University of Oregon. I had watched him compete for Springfield High School when he claimed a state title in the mile run. Then I met and got to know him when we were in some of the same army ROTC classes.

Finally, I found myself doing some track and field coverage for the *Daily Emerald*, the UO student newspaper, in 1953–54 and stumbling into the birth of the school's distance-running tradition under coach Bill Bowerman. I had no clue at the time that it was a tradition that would become renowned first regionally, then nationally and then internationally.

And it officially came off the launching pad in 1954, when Dellinger thought that his successful sophomore season was over after he won the Pacific Coast Conference mile title in 4:14.8, his personal best to that point. He had no idea that he was about to become a national champion and set in motion the tradition that Bowerman had mapped out in his creative mind.

Legendary names, none bigger to the fans than Steve Prefontaine, would follow. Included were Jim Bailey, Dyrol Burleson, Jim Grelle, Kenny Moore, Alberto Salazar, Roscoe Divine, Rudy Chapa, Arne Kvalheim, Matt Centrowitz (and son Matthew years later), Archie San Romani, Keith Forman, Galen Rupp and Andrew Wheating. Records were set in droves, some of them world marks. Rupp even reminded many of the late Prefontaine when his gutty effort earned him a silver medal in the 10,000 meters at the 2012 Olympic Games in London.

Oregon coach Bill Dellinger is carried on the shoulders of team members after the Ducks won a track and field championship. *Courtesy of UO Athletics Media Relations.*

Hayward Field, the Ducks' former football home—with the track and field team using it for spring meets—eventually became strictly a track and field facility. It was renovated several times, eventually blossoming into a showpiece site capable of being host to national and international events.

As for Dellinger, I got to know him better after I moved on to my post-college sportswriting career and he went into teaching and coaching, eventually becoming an assistant to Bowerman and later the Ducks' head coach himself when Bowerman retired in 1972.

Anyway, I had an interview with Dellinger in 1962, when he was a coach/teacher at Thurston High School, not far from Hayward Field, where he still was training. In it, we discussed in detail just what happened in the spring of 1954 when he thought his season was over but, instead, became Bowerman's choice to put his coaching methods for distance runners in the national spotlight.

Dellinger described how he was packing his gear and anticipating a break from competition when teammate Ken Reiser approached him.

"Hey, don't put that stuff away," Reiser said. "Bowerman wants you to run in the NCAA meet."

"At first, I thought Reiser was kidding," Dellinger said. "When I saw that he wasn't, I figured Bowerman must be off his rocker. Frankly, I didn't think I had a chance in the world to stay with the best milers in the country."

What followed is well known among devoted followers of track and field in the Pacific Northwest. Dellinger, pessimism and all, did more than "stay

One-on-one coaching was a strength of Bill Dellinger, here advising a member of the women's team. *Courtesy of UO Athletics Media Relations.*

with" the nation's best in the meet in Ann Arbor, Michigan. He ran them right into a state of shock with a final lap of 0:56.0 and won the race in 4:13.8, an excellent time in those days. His win came three weeks after England's Roger Bannister became the first runner to break the mile's four-minute barrier with his historic 3:59.4 clocking.

"I remember the day (of the NCAA race) well," Dellinger said. "It was muggy hot, not a good day at all for running. There was a thermometer near the track, and it read ninety-eight degrees. Bowerman had kept telling me that I had a good chance to win. I never did believe him until I hit the finish tape. I was convinced that I was going to be thoroughly outclassed that day."

For three of the race's four laps, it did appear as if Dellinger might be in over his head. He was dead last in the field of eighteen at the halfway point. He still was twelfth heading into the final lap. Even Bowerman's optimism must have wavered.

"As we went around the first turn on the last lap, I went into my kick and started counting the guys in front of me," Dellinger said. "I was thinking in terms of getting up to sixth place."

About halfway up the backstretch, he counted five runners still ahead of him. With about 220 yards to go, he was fourth.

"That's when I suddenly realized that maybe I did have a chance to win," he said. "Honestly, it was the first time that the possibility had crossed my mind."

Dellinger sprinted past Lew Olive of Army, Lowell Zellers of Indiana and Bill Squires of Notre Dame as the four came out of the final turn. He had a solid five-yard lead over Olive at the finish.

Bowerman had his "trophy win" and the increased interest in distance running at Oregon that he sought. The interest picked up steam in a hurry as Bailey, the surprising Australian with little competitive background, won the NCAA mile in 1955 in 4:05.6, with Dellinger second in 4:06.4.

In May 1956, Bailey and Dellinger were invited to the Coliseum Relays in Los Angeles to run in an invitational mile race. The select field included Australia's John Landy, who recently had joined Bannister as a sub-4:00.0 miler. Bailey edged Landy 3:58.6 to 3:58.7 to become the first runner to break 4:00.0 on American soil. Dellinger finished fourth, in 4:08.8, and began to realize that his specialty for the future would be longer races.

All the while, the buzz was on that Oregon had something special going with distance running. Recruiting became easier. Crowds at Hayward Field increased dramatically. Success and records followed almost monotonously.

Dellinger, who set seven American and two world records in distance races from 1956 to 1959, made it to the Olympic Games in the 5,000 meters in 1956 and 1960. He succumbed to the heat at Melbourne in 1956 and to the flu in Rome in 1960. Finally, in 1964 in Tokyo, he made it to the medal stand, claiming the bronze behind Bob Schul and Harold Norpoth after his go-for-broke surge had him in the lead heading into the final lap.

Bill Dellinger shakes hands with distance runner Steve Prefontaine, whom he helped recruit to Oregon while an assistant coach. *Courtesy of UO Athletics Media Relations.*

Still, in that 1962 interview, Dellinger downplayed his importance in being the harbinger of Oregon's distance-running tradition.

"Give Bowerman the credit," he said. "He deserves it. People seem to forget that he was a great distance coach before I came along. He had a fine coaching reputation. Why, when I finished high school, I decided to go to Oregon simply because Bowerman was the coach there. Had he been at Oregon State, instead, I would have gone there."

His modesty was admirable, but the fact is that Dellinger's thrilling NCAA win in 1954 started it all.

And of course, Dellinger continued Bowerman's tradition in a twenty-five-year reign as Oregon's head coach, claiming five NCAA championships and compiling a 134-29 record in dual meets. In 2001, he even joined Bowerman, his mentor, as a member of the National Track and Field Hall of Fame.

When Dellinger was selected for the latter honor, I couldn't help but contemplate how far he had come from the days in those tedious army ROTC classes.

# 4

# Bradley's Big Game

Bill Bradley trotted onto the court to mild applause during player introductions on that March night in 1965 in Portland's Memorial Coliseum. He went through the motions of encouraging his Princeton University teammates as the Tigers prepared to face an injury- and academic-depleted Wichita State team in the consolation game of NCAA basketball's Final Four.

"This game is a waste of time," one early arriving writer said in the press section. "It's going to be a yawner." Or, in other words, an agonizing prelude to the classic showdown for the championship between defending titlist UCLA and favored Michigan.

In that one, it would be John Wooden's small but deceptively quick Bruins, epitomized by left-hander Gail Goodrich, against the burly Wolverines, led by all-around star Cazzie Russell.

A mouthy San Francisco writer loudly offered to bet on the Bruins with anyone who wanted to back Michigan. He got several takers, mostly writers from the East and Midwest, and was all smiles after UCLA, behind Goodrich's forty-two points, scored a resounding 91–80 victory.

Now back to Bradley and the consolation game. My assignment that night was to do a sidebar story for the *Oregonian* on the championship game and to "throw in a couple of paragraphs" on the Princeton–Wichita State prelude.

But a strange thing happened. While the Tigers were toying with the Shockers, Bradley began putting on a shooting exhibition that eventually drove the sellout crowd of nearly thirteen thousand into a frenzy. He had nineteen points at halftime, and Princeton led 53–39. There was nothing too alarming about that because Bradley averaged just over thirty points per game for his Princeton career. But after the intermission, his scoring output turned into an avalanche.

Before the game, it turned out, Princeton coach Butch van Breda Kolff had called Bradley, a senior, aside and told him, "This is your last (college) game. Go out there and shoot the ball."

Still, Bradley, always a team player, couldn't understand why his teammates kept passing up good shots in the second half to get the ball to him.

During a timeout, Bradley overheard talk in his team's huddle of a record. He thought he had it figured out. The Princeton single-game scoring record was 112, and it looked as if the Tigers might have a shot at it.

But that wasn't it at all. Van Breda Kolff wanted Bradley to break Oscar Robertson's single-game NCAA tournament record at the time of fifty-six points. He knew better than to share his thinking with Bradley. He figured the team-oriented All-American would have balked. So he had told the other players of his goal but kept his six-foot-five star in the dark.

All the while, spectators realized that they were seeing something special and cheered louder by the minute. When Princeton called another timeout with just under four minutes to go, Bradley had forty-six points. Van Breda Kolff asked him, as team captain, to go to the scorer's table to check on the team's foul situation. Bradley thought it was an odd request with the Tigers so far in front. But while he was away, van Breda Kolff was busy filling his teammates in on the situation.

"After that timeout, coach van Breda Kolff and my teammates kept shouting at me to shoot," Bradley said after the game. "It seemed really strange. Everybody just kept passing the ball to me whether I was open or not."

Bradley hit a couple of jumpers from the left side and another from the top of the key. He even nailed a sweeping hook shot from along the baseline. Finally, another jumper gave him fifty-eight points and the record he knew nothing about. The game's final minute was ticking away, and van Breda Kolff bellowed to one of his players to foul in order to stop the clock.

Then he substituted for Bradley, who appeared more bewildered than overwhelmed by the standing ovation. When he got to the sideline, he learned what all the excitement was about. And it wasn't because the Tigers were about to break that school scoring record with their 118–82 victory. Bradley's final statistics were otherworldly—twenty-two of twenty-nine field goals and fourteen of fifteen free throws.

During a lull in the second half, I had called my editor, and it was quickly determined that I would be doing a lot more than "throwing in a couple of paragraphs" on this consolation game.

Later, in the locker room, I asked Bradley, who later was selected as the Final Four's most outstanding player, how it felt to break a record held by Robertson. "I always feel flattered when someone mentions me in a comparison with Robertson," he replied softly. "I don't know what to say other than that."

At one point, he thought back to the semifinals when Princeton had lost to Michigan 93–76. "It's just too bad that this all didn't happen one game sooner," he said.

Bradley, who had played on the U.S. team that won a basketball gold medal at the 1964 Tokyo Olympics, also shared some thoughts on his future. A Rhodes Scholar, he was headed to Oxford. He said there was "not much chance" that he would change his mind and play in the NBA instead.

Of course, his two years abroad and some European pro basketball play only delayed his start in the NBA. "In the past two years, I've discovered something that I always expected—I love the game of basketball too much to give it up," he told the *Daily Princetonian*. So he returned to the United States and signed with the New York Knicks, playing on their championship teams of 1970 and 1973. In a ten-year NBA career, he averaged 12.4 points in regular-season play and 12.9 in ninety-five playoff games.

Later, as a Democrat, he served three terms as a U.S. senator from New Jersey, and in 2000, he ran unsuccessfully for the Democratic presidential nomination, losing to Al Gore.

The latter developments made me think back to 1965, when I had asked Bradley about rumors that he was planning to get into politics and had designs on running for the Senate and perhaps even for president.

He laughed then and said, "It's a little presumptuous to say I might run for president."

As it turned out, not so presumptuous after all.

## 5

# Trail Blazing to a Title

Herm Gilliam had begrudgingly bought into Portland coach Jack Ramsay's team philosophy all season long, but on this Sunday afternoon at the Forum in Los Angeles, he saw the need to provide some of his best one-on-one moves. I got the feeling that he had been eagerly waiting for such an opportunity.

It was the 1977 NBA Playoffs, the Portland Trail Blazers against the favored Lakers in the Western Conference Finals. The Blazers already were one-up in the series after being in command virtually all the way in a 121–109 win two days earlier at the Forum. Even LA coach Jerry West admitted that this might be a "must-win" game for his team.

The Lakers, who had won thirty-seven of forty-one home games in the regular season, got in front late, 91–84. On the sideline, a fan next to the Blazers' bench was going crazy, jumping up and down, screaming at the officials—showing anything but Hollywood cool.

Portland forward Lloyd Neal, sitting closest to the fan, asked a teammate, "Who is that clown?" He was told that it was actor Jack Nicholson, star of the acclaimed movie *One Flew Over the Cuckoo's Nest.*

Meanwhile, Gilliam, sometimes called "The Trickster" by teammates for his baffling array of moves, was using every weapon in his offensive arsenal to rally the Blazers. I'd never seen him play so spectacularly and never would again. He simply was magnificent, with fourteen of his twenty-four points in the fourth quarter as Portland won 99–97 and took a two-up series lead.

Maurice Lucas of Portland Trail Blazers gives chase as Philadelphia's George McGinnis makes a move in the 1977 NBA title series. *Photo by Roger Jensen.*

Moments after the final buzzer, Neal stepped in front of Nicholson and said, "How's you like that Mr. Cuckoo Man?" Nearby teammates cracked up, and even Nicholson seemed to be amused.

I considered that game-two win a watershed moment for the Blazers, setting up a trip to the NBA Finals. Predictably, Ramsay expressed words of caution, but I had little doubt that Portland would win the next two games in its home Memorial Coliseum and claim a stunning sweep. The Blazers did, but it didn't come as easily as I anticipated.

The Lakers' Kareem Abdul-Jabbar, so dominant when the mood struck him, did his best to stand in the way. But Blazers center Bill Walton, occasionally smiling and patting Kareem on the back, neutralized him enough that Portland prevailed 102–97 and 105–101.

Walton's joviality with Abdul-Jabbar puzzled me, and after the series, I asked him about the seemingly friendly exchanges. Walton gave me a knowing look and said, "I was just telling Kareem how great he was playing. The last thing you want to do against him is make him mad."

It was time for the Blazers to challenge the Eastern Conference champion, and I feared a problem brewing. Because of their sweep of the Lakers, the Blazers faced nine days off before playing the winner of the Philadelphia-Houston series in the title matchup. The sports landscape is full of stories of rested teams not being ready when matched against opponents who are fatigued but riding momentum.

Trail Blazers coach Jack Ramsay (left) and assistant Jack McKinney show game faces while watching action in 1977 game. *Photo by Roger Jensen.*

Finally, Philadelphia edged Houston 112–109 in the sixth game to win the Eastern Conference series.

During the long break before the first two games of the finals at the Spectrum in Philadelphia, I did a story on the power forward matchup of the Blazers' Maurice Lucas and the 76ers' George McGinnis, the latter mired in a prolonged shooting slump.

"It always has been pretty physical between us," Lucas said. "I don't imagine it will be much different this time."

Ramsay, who scouted the 76ers' clincher against the Rockets, seemed confident enough, even with guard Dave Twardzik limited by an ankle sprain and Lucas trying to shake off a stomach virus. "I think we are ready," the coach said. I had my doubts because of the long layoff.

For another story, I talked to Golden State forward Rick Barry, who would be working the finals as a TV analyst for CBS.

"The Blazers play intelligently, and they move well without the ball, which is a big plus," he said. "Then there is Bill Walton. He does so many things for them. I like to call him the orchestrator of it all." Oddly, after his lofty praise of the Blazers, Barry picked Philadelphia to win the series.

On the other side, I was amused that 76ers coach Gene Shue closed his practices to the media on the two days before the Sunday opener. "There will be some new wrinkles for Portland," he said of his seemingly over-cautious approach. "You writers may not recognize them, but there will be some." Shue's needle obviously was out for the local media.

Then came the first two games of the series, and the Blazers looked as out of sorts as I had seen them all season. They committed an outlandish thirty-four turnovers in game one and lost 107–101. It wasn't as close as the score indicated. To add insult, Julius Erving and Doug Collins of the 76ers, who had combined for sixty-three points, did an impromptu dance off the court at the finish.

The second game, three days later, was even worse as the Blazers had twenty-nine more turnovers and shot a woeful .356 from the field. They were outclassed 107–89, and I had difficulty understanding what was wrong. Why, I wondered, was Shue's "new wrinkle"—having center Caldwell Jones bring the ball up court to defuse Portland's pressing tactics—making such a difference?

There also was a nonsensical brawl with just over five minutes remaining in game two and the 76ers coasting with a 96–76 lead. It got its start when Philadelphia center Darryl Dawkins threw the Blazers' Bob Gross to the floor while pulling down a rebound. Gross bounced up and said something that prompted Dawkins to go after him. Collins, trying to be a peacemaker, grabbed hold of Gross. Dawkins unleashed a left hook, but Gross dodged it, and the blow struck Collins.

Then Lucas came running and threw a punch that hit Dawkins on the back of the head. Amazingly, the blow didn't seem to faze the player who had Chocolate Thunder among his nicknames. Dawkins and Lucas squared off and missed with a couple of poorly aimed punches before being restrained.

Meanwhile, in an ugly and scary scene, the floor was inundated by coaches, bench players and more than one hundred fans who tried to get in on the action. One of the fans went after a Portland player and was grabbed and pummeled by Blazers assistant coach Jack McKinney.

Finally, order was restored. Dawkins and Lucas were ejected, and Collins eventually had to have stitches for a cut on his forehead. "I can't believe it," Collins said. "I'm trying to help the guy [Dawkins], and he ends up hitting me."

Gross declined to say at the time what he had said that so annoyed Dawkins. He still remains mum about it.

"When he threw me down, it was kind of like the last straw after he had done some other stuff to me," he said several years after the incident. "I

Portland's Bob Gross, a star of the Trail Blazers' NBA title run in 1977, hooks a pass over Chicago's Norm Van Lier in a first-round game. *Photo by Roger Jensen.*

jumped up and said something that was very offensive to him. I'm not going to say what it was, but it wasn't something you would have wanted to publish."

After game two, I was working on my story in the media room when Nick Bertram, another *Oregonian* writer working on our coverage, came back from the Philadelphia locker room and tapped me on the shoulder. "You won't believe what happened down there," he said. He then described how an infuriated and incredibly strong Dawkins had caved in the metal side of a toilet stall and tore the door to the stall from its hinges. He apparently didn't take kindly to a lack of support from teammates in the mêlée.

I was shocked by what had happened in those first two games and couldn't help but wonder if the Blazers could recover from such a bumbling start. Consequently, I was curious to see how they reacted on the commercial flight back to Portland the next morning.

What I saw was encouraging. The players were quiet and had none of the jovial exchanges that I had seen from them so often on flights. After reading stories on the game in Philadelphia newspapers, I noticed some of the Blazers crumpling the papers and throwing them on the floor. I didn't need a psychiatrist to tell me that an inner rage was eating away at them. I doubted that focus would be a problem for games three and four at the Coliseum.

Later that day, NBA commissioner Larry O'Brien announced that Lucas and Dawkins would be fined $2,500 each for their part in the brawl, the largest monetary penalty issued to a player by the NBA at the time.

Portland's problems in the first two games were obvious. The Blazers were careless with the ball, causing surplus turnovers. They shot too quickly instead of working through options on their plays. They didn't work hard enough at getting into their running game. I think Ramsay was embarrassed. I know that he was frustrated.

Simply put, the Blazers hadn't yet played their usual high-octane game in the series, the one that produced a 146–104 thrashing of the 76ers in an early meeting of the regular season. The deadline for getting back to that type of play was at hand if their improbable championship dream was to be realized.

Then, in a seeming instant, it happened. Shue's strategy, which had worked so well in Philadelphia, backfired in Portland as the Blazers increased their defensive pressure behind the leadership of guards Lionel Hollins and Johnny Davis. They ran at will, took their time in half-court situations and capitalized on selfless team play.

Part of the turnaround came during player introductions before game three. When Lucas's name was announced, he took a detour and trotted toward the Philadelphia bench. I heard some gasps from spectators as Lucas approached Dawkins. Then there was massive applause as Lucas, frequently called "The Enforcer," shook Dawkins's hand.

"I just wanted to let Darryl know that I was sorry for what happened and that I had no hard feelings," Lucas said. "No words were spoken."

Games three and four were similar. The Blazers won 129–107 and 130–98—a rout and an even bigger rout. I loved the story lead of Bill Livingston of the *Philadelphia Inquirer* after game four: "The Portland Trail Blazers are winning the NBA title, two to two."

Lucas and Walton led the way in points and rebounds in the two games, and the Blazers had no trouble after a pivotal sequence early in the fourth quarter of game three. Gross lofted a lob pass to Walton from the right wing. Walton lost his balance going up but managed to hang in the air long enough to tip the ball over the rim and in before falling to the court.

Walton had just gotten back on his feet when he spotted Twardzik—who had made a steal—looking his way. This time he took the lob with both hands and dunked. Spectators went bananas as the Portland lead ballooned from four to eight points. It was no contest after that.

"I've never seen anything like that [sequence] in my life," said 76ers guard Henry Bibby, a former teammate of Walton at UCLA.

A 41–21 surge in the third quarter turned game four into a laugher. The Blazers were back to being their free-wheeling selves. I could see the swagger in their eyes and with their smiles. I thought Gross, who was on his way to compiling an amazing shooting percentage in the series, summed up the team's outlook best. "We captured the flow of our game tonight," he said. "Now we want to take it back to Philadelphia with us."

The Blazers did just that, cruising into a 79–60 lead at the Spectrum with a 26–8 burst in the third quarter. Then they staved off a too-little-too-late Philadelphia rally for a 110–104 victory that robbed the 76ers of their home court advantage.

Gross, spelled off the bench by Corky Calhoun and Larry Steele, again was splendid with twenty-five points on ten-of-thirteen shooting while defensively doing his best to keep Erving from taking over the game. The acrobatic Erving was getting his points, but he must have felt as if he were fighting off a trio of buzzing yellow jackets that refused to be shooed away.

There also was an amusing confrontation the day before game five when the Blazers arrived at the Spectrum for their scheduled 1:00 p.m.

Bill Walton of the Trail Blazers (left) battles for position with Chicago's Artis Gilmore in an opening-round game of the 1977 NBA Playoffs. *Photo by Roger Jensen.*

practice. The 76ers' practice was supposed to end at 1:00 p.m., but Shue kept his players on the court and sent word to Ramsay that he wanted another fifteen minutes.

A miffed Ramsay declined and herded his players onto the court at exactly 1:00 p.m. "I wouldn't think of holding up another team's scheduled practice," he said, his chin jutting out.

My take was that there was no love lost between Ramsay and Shue. Maybe respect was lacking on both sides. Or maybe it was just a case of shared embarrassment—Ramsay after the first two games and Shue after the next two.

Anyway, when the Blazers came onto the court for their practice, the 76ers considered it an intrusion and reacted negatively. "To hell with that, they can't do it," Bibby said to Shue. Reserve forward Joe Bryant said, "I can't believe it. They are kicking us off our own floor."

Finally, a compromise was reached. While the Blazers did their pre-workout stretching at one end of the arena, the 76ers ran through another ten minutes of drills at the other.

I had an interesting experience after game five, which was played on a Friday night. Because of the tight scheduling before game six in Portland on

Sunday, the NBA and Blazers management arranged for a chartered team flight home shortly after the game. I couldn't make it because of stories I had to write. So John White, Portland's director of media relations, arranged for me to be on the 76ers' charter the next day.

What I observed on that flight was a bedraggled-looking group of Philadelphia players, some accompanied by girlfriends. It didn't look anything like a team that had a chance to come back and win the series. Shortly after takeoff, a stewardess announced that the movie *Rocky*, a big hit at the time, would be shown. I'm sure Shue hoped that Sylvester Stallone, in his underdog boxing role, would light a fire under his players.

But when it came time for the movie, *The Cassandra Crossing* flashed onto screens, and there was grumbling and laughter. Someone had gotten the tapes in the wrong containers. Rocky Balboa was somewhere else.

Back in Portland, I learned that more than five thousand fans had been waiting to greet the Blazers at the airport that morning. And the charter hadn't arrived until 4:30 a.m., Portland time. An affliction that had been branded as "Blazermania" was spreading fast.

McKinney told me about his exchange with one of those fans: "Three fellows, who were pretty well inebriated, slapped hands with me as I came off the plane. I asked one of them how long they had been waiting. He replied: 'How long has the game been over?' Amazing."

There was another touch of controversy before game six. O'Brien called Harry Glickman, the Blazers' executive vice-president, and said that CBS wanted a 10:30 a.m. tipoff so the game wouldn't overlap with the network's showing of the Kemper Open golf tournament. After a brief discussion, Glickman took a stand against an unnatural morning start for what he described as "the most important game in franchise history."

He finally told O'Brien, "You can start the telecast at ten thirty if you want but the Trail Blazers won't be there until noon." He got his way, and the game was scheduled for a noon tipoff. Then CBS got even by making a quick switch to the golf tournament after the game, declining to provide a scheduled post-game show.

When the game commenced, the 76ers quickly showed that it was a miscalculation to think they would be easy pickings after three straight losses. They kept the Blazers from putting together one of their patented early spurts, and McGinnis shook off his shooting slump by sinking his first three shots. It was 27–27 after the first quarter and 40–40 five minutes into the second.

Then the Blazers built a fifteen-point lead before settling for a 67–55 halftime edge. Hollins, who had been outplayed by Collins early in the series,

Trail Blazers founder Harry Glickman, above at the 1971 NBA draft, squelched CBS's bid for a morning start for game six of the 1977 NBA Finals. *Portland Trail Blazers archive photo.*

led the way. Suddenly, his fast-paced game was back, and he was dominating the 76ers' guard.

Still, Philadelphia was far from finished as Erving and McGinnis, who combined for sixty-eight points, gave Portland plenty of cause for anxiety. When the Blazers' offense fizzled late in the game, the 76ers rallied, closing their deficit to 109–107 on McGinnis's outside jumper with eighteen seconds left. That was followed by two incidents, a non-call by the officials and a Portland defensive lapse, which could have changed both the game's outcome and NBA history.

As the Blazers tried to run out the clock, Gross was trapped on the sideline, just a few feet in front of my press row seat. I had an up-close view as he cleverly kept moving the ball away from the groping hands of two 76ers. He was fouled at least twice, and I couldn't believe there was no whistle. Finally, there was a whistle, and McGinnis was given a jump ball opportunity with Gross. The taller McGinnis won the tip.

Apprehension enveloped the record Coliseum crowd of 12,951 as the 76ers moved to the attack. Erving hurried an outside jumper that missed. Lloyd Free rebounded but had his baseline jumper blocked out of bounds by Gross. Five seconds remained as Philadelphia inbounded from under the basket. Then came the defensive lapse as Lucas lost track of McGinnis, who worked clear for a fifteen-footer from the key.

There was a deafening roar as the ball bounced off the rim. The noise escalated when Walton tipped the rebound to rookie Davis, who headed down court as the clock ran out. Bedlam followed with celebrating spectators bursting onto the court. Portland, with its 109–107 win, had become the first team in NBA history to win the championship series four to two after losing the first two games.

Walton, selected as the series' most valuable player, finished game six with awe-inspiring numbers: Twenty points, twenty-three rebounds, seven assists and eight blocked shots. Gross added twenty-four points while sinking twelve of sixteen field goal attempts, giving him a torrid .667 shooting percentage for the series on forty-six of sixty-nine.

Downtown Portland was the site of one big party that night with traffic at a virtual standstill. The city undoubtedly led the nation in hangovers the next day when estimates were as high as 250,000 attendees for a parade honoring the Blazers.

It had been some kind of title run by a young and sometimes naïve team. I couldn't help but reflect on Twardzik doing a hula dance in front of the Portland bench at the end of the first-round series with Chicago, signaling to his wife that there would be a family trip to Hawaii with some of his playoff bonus money.

Then there was Steele, who, after the Chicago series, contemplated buying a new car, a Chevrolet. After Denver fell in the second round, he said he planned an upgrade to a Buick. After the Lakers were swept, he began thinking about a Volvo. Finally, after the championship was won, he admitted to looking at a BMW before deciding just to put his playoff money in a bank.

Later, after the parade, I worked at the *Oregonian* on a follow-up story. At one point, I leaned back in my chair and took a moment to marvel at how cool it had been to be part of the whole thing.

# 6

# Recollections of Luke

Maurice Lucas was in good spirits that fall day in 2009. He was on hand for a media indoctrination session for players and coaches conducted by the NBA and the Portland Trail Blazers. He looked great, even robust. He seemingly had made a successful recovery from bladder cancer surgery the previous April.

"Oh, boy, here comes trouble," Lucas said when he saw me approaching. Of course, I had interviewed him dozens of times back when I was covering Portland's NBA championship team of 1977 for the *Oregonian* and he was doing his thing as the feisty power forward who often was called "The Enforcer." We shook hands—his enormous paw engulfing mine—and I told him he looked healthy enough to play some hoops.

"I'm not quite ready for that, but I feel great," he said. "I'm ready to go back to work [as an assistant coach for the Blazers under Nate McMillan]."

We talked about old times, and naturally, the subject of his fight with Darryl Dawkins in the second game of the 1977 NBA Finals between the Blazers and the Philadelphia 76ers came up.

"The way it is set up today, I would have been toast for that one," he said. "The suspension would have been a long one—really long."

Lucas then laughed and rolled his eyes when reminded about another incident that season, this one in a first-round playoff series against the Chicago Bulls.

It was the opening game of a best-of-three series, and Lucas had a dominant game, scoring twenty-nine points on fourteen-of-seventeen shooting as

Portland's Maurice Lucas drives against Philadelphia's George McGinnis in the 1977 NBA Finals. *Photo by Roger Jensen.*

Portland pulled away late for a 96–83 victory in packed Memorial Coliseum. When I suggested that he was lucky to be around at the finish of that one, he just smiled and said, "I can't deny that."

There was a strike of NBA referees at the time, and the league temporarily was using replacement officials. Mike Eggers and Paul Wilson worked this game, and their inexperience showed with a surplus of foul calls. Lucas finally lost his cool with 9:36 remaining and the Blazers leading 75–70. Eggers hit him with a technical foul for protesting a call.

Instead of backing off, a furious Lucas walked up to Eggers and yanked the whistle from his mouth. Amazingly, he got away with it.

"Let me tell you a story about that," Lucas said. "Years later, I was watching one of my sons play in a youth league. After the game, the referee came over and said, 'Do you remember me?' I was stumped. Well, it was Mike Eggers. We had a nice visit and laughed about what had happened between us."

That turned out to be the last time I visited with Lucas. Sadly, his cancer returned, forcing him to resign his coaching position after the 2009–10 season. He was fifty-eight when he died on October 31, 2010.

Lucas was one of my favorite Blazers, almost always patient and willing to put up with a writer's request. He liked to joke with you, but he was frank with answers, most of the time even to uncomfortable questions.

The Blazers traded Geoff Petrie and Steve Hawes to the Atlanta Hawks to get the second pick in the 1976 dispersal draft of the folding American Basketball Association. They used it to select Lucas. They also chose a brash twenty-year-old, Moses Malone, with the fifth pick.

Malone played with the Blazers through the 1976–77 exhibition season, rotating with Lucas and center Bill Walton and showing considerable talent and potential. Then, suddenly, Malone was traded to Buffalo for a first-round draft pick and cash, eventually ending up with Houston and becoming a star.

I talked to Lucas the day after Malone's departure, and he obviously was distressed. I asked him what was bothering him. "I miss Mo," he replied. Silence followed.

Blazers management gave as reasons for the trade that it couldn't afford to keep Malone and that it feared a chemistry breakdown because both Malone and Walton were adamant about wanting to start.

Although, diplomatically, he didn't spell it out, the six-foot-nine Lucas knew that a big three of himself, Walton and Malone could have made the

Bill Walton puts up a left-handed shot against Chicago in the 1977 NBA Playoffs as teammate Maurice Lucas (center) takes a rebounding position. *Photo by Roger Jensen.*

Blazers an even more powerful team. In hindsight, keeping Malone might have allowed coach Jack Ramsay to limit Walton's minutes and perhaps could have staved off his later demise with injuries.

The wisdom of the trade, of course, was brought into revealing focus a few days after it was completed when Buffalo traded Malone to Houston for two first-round draft picks.

Years later, in an interview with editor Matt Love for the book *Red Hot and Rollin'* (Nestucca Spit Press, 2007), Lucas made his feelings about the Malone trade quite clear, saying, "One of the biggest mistakes they [the Blazers] ever made was getting rid of Moses."

The Malone trade, though, was forgotten for the most part as Portland suddenly became a contender and eventually a champion with a four-to-two series win over the 76ers.

Lucas's enforcer role actually was by appointment, although he had a running start on the reputation after decking seven-foot-two Artis Gilmore in an ABA game.

Ramsay hadn't met Lucas at the time of his hiring to replace fired Lenny Wilkens as Blazers coach in 1976. So one of his first orders of business was to travel to upstate New York to visit with him at a basketball camp.

"I told Luke that I was concerned that Portland had a reputation as a soft team," Ramsay recalled. "I said, 'I would like you to be our tough guy, to have the other players' backs.' As I laid out my plan, his smile got wider and there was a twinkle in his eyes. He said, 'I can do that.' And he did a very good job at it."

In the championship season, Lucas led the Blazers in scoring both for the regular season (20.2) and the playoffs (21.2). And he did that within the strong team framework that Ramsay established. I was pleasantly surprised at how well he lived up to the acclaim that he had gotten for leading Marquette to an NCAA runner-up finish to North Carolina State in 1974.

"He was the strength and heart of our championship team," Ramsay said.

Walton, on a college game telecast after Lucas's death, described him as "the best teammate I ever had."

There were occasions, though, when Lucas couldn't resist varying his role within Ramsay's team-oriented offense. One of those came in the opening game of the second-round playoff series against the Nuggets in Denver. The Nuggets had taken a 100–99 lead when Ramsay called a timeout with twenty seconds remaining to set up a play.

"The plan was for Luke to get the ball and pass it to [Dave] Twardzik to set up a backdoor play," Ramsay said. "But Luke just took the ball and made his own play [resulting in a spinning eight-foot jumper that he sank over the Nuggets' Dan Issel]. I think it was the only time all night that we resorted to a one-on-one play, and I loved it."

The Blazers' 101–100 win took away Denver's home court advantage and set up a four-to-two series win.

Denver coach Larry Brown took his team to the Air Force Academy early in that series to make some "secret" changes to combat Lucas. Paul Silas, the former Boston Celtic, was moved into the starting lineup with his major responsibility to guard Lucas. The strategy failed as Lucas continued to dominate the Nuggets.

I interviewed Silas about Lucas before game five of the series. He was candid with me. "It's difficult for me to guard him," he said. "He is taller and he has that high release with his jump shot. He is the premier power forward in the game."

Among my favorite quotes about Lucas was one from Mike Dunleavy, later a coach in the NBA but a reserve guard for the 76ers in 1976–77. "Maurice treats all of us like [Humphrey] Bogart treated his women—with the back of his hand," Dunleavy said.

Maurice Lucas (right) shakes hands with Harry Glickman as his jersey is retired in 1988. Club owner Paul Allen and Lucas's family share the moment. *Portland Trail Blazers archive photo.*

One of my most enjoyable interviews with Lucas came on a day when I got him to talk about his background. He told me how he had been a good swimmer and loved the sport as a kid before his older brother, Clifford, talked him into concentrating on basketball at Schenley High School in Pittsburgh, Pennsylvania.

"Clifford told me I wasn't going to get a college scholarship as a swimmer and that I needed to concentrate on basketball," Lucas said.

He actually started out as a six-foot guard at Schenley. "Believe it or not, I grew six and one-half inches in the summer and fall after my sophomore year," he said. "That changed my whole outlook."

Lucas, who often had a scowl that could melt ice on the basketball court, was a fraud in a way. Off the court, he was a happy-go-lucky jester with a smile that invigorated those around him. He just didn't want to be known to opponents as a nice guy.

"I have to play a physical game to be at my best, so sometimes guys confront me," he told me. "I don't mind being the villain. I love it."

It didn't take long for Portland fans to fall for Lucas. Their affection showed when they chanted "Luuuke" when he was introduced before games and at other times.

That was in sharp contrast to the boos and catcalls that he received at many other NBA arenas. He seemed to thrive on the jeers. Interestingly, the Portland fans didn't lose their fondness for him late in his career when he played for other teams before returning to the Blazers.

Finally, it seemed only fitting at Lucas's memorial service—held in the Coliseum where he had so many great moments and had his number retired—that those in attendance stood and chanted "Luuuke" to close the ceremony. I'm sure it was my imagination, but I thought I heard an echo.

# 7

# The Sweet Scent of Roses

The outcome of the 2012 Rose Bowl football game was hanging in the balance. Then came a most improbable play that sent the University of Oregon on the way to a 45–38 victory over Wisconsin. As a longtime and ardent follower of the Rose Bowl, I couldn't help but think that the play, because of the unusual way it unfolded, would claim some prominence in the lore of an annual game that is often referred to as the "Granddaddy" of football's post-season.

It happened this way, and those watching on TV were provided with much better viewing of it than most of those in the famed stadium in Pasadena, California. History will record it as a story of a football that wobbled slightly but seemed to stick to the turf as if glued in place.

With slightly more than four minutes remaining, Wisconsin quarterback Russell Wilson was guiding his team downfield to what loomed as a tying touchdown, especially after he completed a sideline pass to Jared Abbrederis. But Oregon's Terrance Mitchell knocked the ball out of the receiver's grasp. Then, in a freakish scene, the ball dropped behind Abbrederis and, instead of taking a typical crazy bounce, simply settled inches from the sideline on the Ducks' side of the field. Seemingly, the only ones unaware of the ball's location were nearby Badgers, including Abbrederis.

A few feet away, Oregon coach Chip Kelly jumped up and down frantically, screaming for one of his players to fall on the fumbled ball. He jumped the highest when UO linebacker Michael Clay finally pounced on it at the Ducks' twenty-seven-yard line, barely keeping it in the field of play. Oregon had staved off Wisconsin's last best chance to erase its deficit.

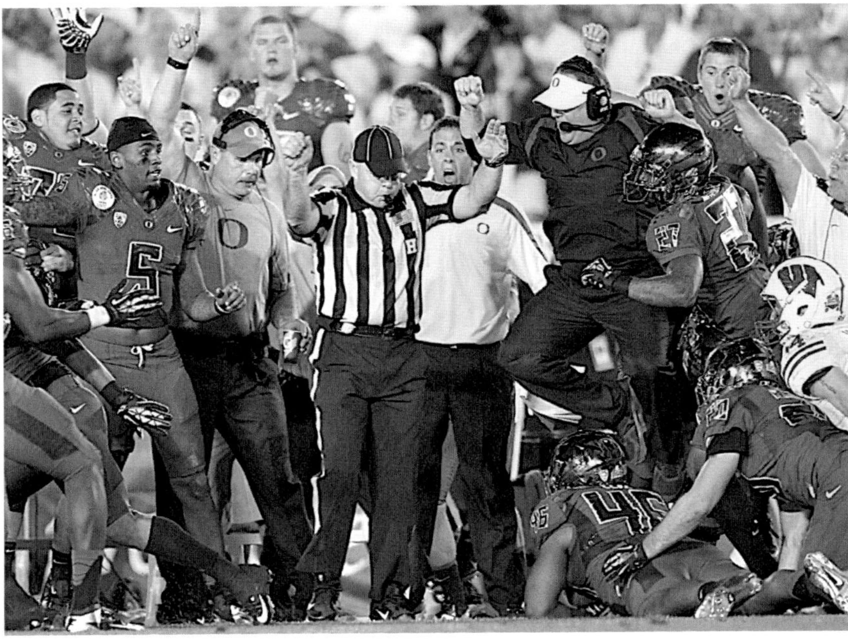

Michael Clay recovers a fumble as Oregon coach Chip Kelly jumps for joy during the Ducks's 45–38 win over Wisconsin in the 2012 Rose Bowl. *Photo by Thomas Boyd/*Oregonian.

Being an Oregon alum, I was delighted that the Ducks had claimed the school's first Rose Bowl win in ninety-five years. But my emotional involvement went much deeper because the Rose Bowl game had become an obsession of mine going back to 1946, when I was in the sixth grade.

Already a sports junkie, I sort of stumbled into the obsession when I was given money by my parents to purchase Christmas gifts for family members. I was weak of will, and part of that money went toward a gift for myself—a book by Los Angeles sportswriter Maxwell Stiles, *The Rose Bowl* (Sportsmaster Publications, 1945). Dog-eared and taped up on its spine, it still is a cherished possession.

Through Stiles's colorful descriptions of each of the games through Southern California's 25–0 rout of Tennessee in 1945, I got a running start at becoming enchanted by the Rose Bowl, its traditions, its pageantry and the many history-making games that have been played in an area of Pasadena called Arroyo Seco.

The games often have turned out to be thrillers similar to the Oregon-Wisconsin matchup. Through 2013, national championship teams had played in the Rose Bowl twenty-nine times.

Still, through research over the years, I have become particularly delighted by details of the games of 1939 and 1942, the first because it had such a fairy-tale finish and the latter because it was the lone Rose Bowl game not played in Pasadena and involved my childhood favorite team, Oregon State.

Duke, with a defensive juggernaut, had an undefeated and unscored-on team going into that 1939 game and appeared to have a hard-earned victory over Howard Jones's Southern California Trojans locked up, leading 3–0 with two minutes remaining. USC had given no indication that it could mount a long drive, let alone score, against the Blue Devils' seemingly impregnable defense.

Then fourth-string quarterback Doyle Nave, who had played in just four of USC's ten games for a total of twenty-eight and a half minutes, was sent onto the field. It was a desperation move suggested to Jones by an assistant coach. All Nave did was complete four consecutive passes to Al Krueger, the last for nineteen yards and a touchdown that gave USC a 7–3 upset win and robbed stunned Duke of its perfect season.

Then, after the 1941 regular season and shortly after the Japanese bombing of Pearl Harbor, it appeared that there would be no Rose Bowl game in 1942. Plans to cancel were made due to the World War II threat of a Japanese attack on the West Coast. But Duke officials saved the day by offering to play host to the game in Durham, North Carolina. Oregon State players, who had battled their way to the Pacific Coast Conference championship despite losses to Southern California and Washington State, breathed a collective sigh of relief.

That Blue Devils team, which had future Oregon State coach Tommy Prothro on its roster, also was unbeaten and was a prohibitive favorite over the Beavers, who had been picked to finish last in the PCC in a pre-season poll. On top of that, the Oregon State team had to spend five days on a train just to get to Durham.

But again, there was a huge upset. Lon Stiner's team from Corvallis, insulted by the lack of respect shown to it, never trailed on the way to a 20–16 victory on a muddy field. The key play, breaking a 14–14 tie late in the third quarter, was a sixty-eight-yard pass connection from Bob Dethman to reserve Gene Gray on which Gray juked his way past the last defender.

Anyway, as I moved into my sportswriting career, eventually at the *Oregonian*, I continued to follow the Rose Bowl with dogged interest, including the 1958 game when Oregon went to Pasadena as about as big an underdog as the Oregon State team had been in 1942. The Ducks got to play in that game against top-ranked Ohio State only because of the no-repeat rule the conference had at the time. Oregon State, which had beaten Oregon 10–7 to tie with the Ducks for the conference title, was thus ineligible.

I wasn't able to attend that game but, on a hunch that it would not be the blowout so many were predicting, I ordered a game program by mail. I was glad that I did. It became a prized souvenir after the Ducks made a gallant bid for an upset before losing to the Buckeyes by the same 10–7 score as they had fallen to Oregon State. A field goal try by Jack Morris that missed by inches was all that kept the Ducks from a tie.

Oregon coach Len Casanova bristled at writers after the game for showing so little respect for his team. One Los Angeles writer even had predicted that the Buckeyes would win 40–0.

Once into my sportswriting career, I longed for the opportunity to cover a Rose Bowl. The opportunity finally came—twice. The experience was intoxicating for someone so into the game's history.

As luck would have it, one of the games I covered had the kind of controversy that the media loves because of the extra interest that is generated. It was 1979, and USC was matched against Michigan. It turned into a slugfest with yardage difficult to come by for both teams. The Trojans, coached by former University of Oregon assistant John Robinson, ended up winning 17–10, but there are those who still feel as if Bo Schembechler's Wolverines were robbed.

To set the stage, USC led 7–3 late in the second quarter and was threatening to score again. The Trojans reached the Michigan three-yard line, and tailback Charles White bulled his way toward the end zone, going airborne at the goal line. But when he was hit by Michigan linebacker Ron Simpkins, the ball popped loose and the Wolverines recovered.

A split second later, line judge Gilbert Marchman gave the touchdown signal while another official signaled that it was a fumble and Michigan recovery. Marchman's call, that White had broken the goal line plane before losing control of the ball, took precedence, referee Paul Kamaski would later explain, because he had the best angle to see the play.

Angry Michigan fans roared their disapproval, and there was confusion and some consternation in the press box as the Trojans lined up to kick off with a 14–3 lead. Most of the writers and broadcasters thought that White had lost the ball before reaching the plane of the goal line. I shrugged when another writer asked me what I thought. I told him I couldn't tell from my vantage point and that I doubted that any of the other media "experts" could, either.

In those days, multiple TV sets were not available in press boxes, and instant replay was a long way from becoming an officiating tool.

Roses dominate the cover of the1958 Rose Bowl program. Oregon lost to heavily favored Ohio State 10–7. *Courtesy of the author.*

So at halftime, I looked up Curt Gowdy of NBC, which was televising the game. I didn't get much clarification. Gowdy said that, after looking at all the angles that the telecast crew had available, he felt that the fumble came before White crossed the goal. "But it was close," he said.

The game ran its course, and then there was more than the usual interest in interviewing the participants.

"It's history now," White said. "I felt I scored and then released the ball."

"Then why did you lie on the ground pounding your fist into the turf before you realized it had been ruled a touchdown?" a writer asked. White suddenly was lost for words.

Simpkins was emphatic that White had lost the ball while he was "considerably short of the goal."

On the other side, USC offensive guard Pat Howell said, "I saw it. I was on the goal line looking up. Charlie was over and then released the ball."

Schembechler, who had been furious when White was ruled to have scored, had cooled off by the time he had his post-game session with the media. "My friend Woody [Ohio State coach Woody Hayes] always has wanted to use instant replay on close calls," he said. "Maybe he's right."

Later, as I wrote my game story, then a follow-up column the next day, I declined to chastise Marchman the way some writers did. I felt that there was a strong chance that he had made the correct call. I still feel that way. After all, he was looking at the play directly down the goal line. There was no vantage point or TV camera view better than that.

I also made prominent mention of a conservative decision by Schembechler that I felt could have influenced the outcome as much as White's controversial touchdown. That was his choice to have the Wolverines punt on fourth down from the USC forty-eight-yard line with just under three minutes remaining. Michigan had three timeouts left but never got the ball back. The Trojans made a pair of first downs, survived Michigan's timeouts and ran out the clock.

It had been another memorable game, and it provided another boost to my already bloated Rose Bowl obsession.

# 8

# Ralph and the Orange Express

Only a couple of minutes remained in the Oregon State basketball team's road game against California in February of 1981, and crusty coach Ralph Miller had his players huddled around him. He was barking out instructions and gesturing with his hands when a curious thing happened. Senior guard Ray Blume casually straightened Miller's necktie, the coach seemingly oblivious to the unexpected grooming.

The Beavers, the nation's top-ranked team, were comfortably in front at the time and went on to a 69–54 win over the Bears. It moved their unbeaten streak to eighteen games.

After the game, I asked Blume what he was doing in that final huddle.

"We had the game won, and I knew the coach was going to be interviewed on TV," he replied with a grin. "I just wanted to make sure he looked nice."

I laughed, and I think Blume knew why. He had admitted to me in an interview for an earlier story that there was a time early in his OSU career when he had been scared to death of Miller.

The incident was a perfect example, though, of how that selfless team, which became popularly known as the "Orange Express," had established a one-for-all attitude that helped make it the team of Miller's dreams. The fact that the Beavers stumbled at the end of the season didn't change that.

Covering that team was right up there as one of my highlight experiences as a sportswriter. It was some kind of trip until Kansas State and Rolando Blackman stunned the Beavers 50–48 in a second-round game of the NCAA playoffs,

Oregon State basketball coach Ralph Miller (left) confers with guard Mark Radford in a 1981 game. *Courtesy of OSU Athletics Media Relations.*

dropping their final record to twenty-six wins and two losses. But more later on that frustrating conclusion.

OSU broadcaster Darrell Aune came up with the Orange Express nickname on the spur of the moment. "It was a game fairly early in the season," he said. "I hadn't planned it or anything like that. It just came out. During a steal and fast break, I blurted 'the Orange Express is rolling.' I kind of liked the sound of it, and I got some good reactions from those working the game with me."

Later that night, Aune told Miller about the name he had inadvertently coined. "I didn't expect to get a ringing endorsement, not from Ralph," Aune said. "But he thought for a moment and then said that he guessed it was OK." It wasn't long before fans up and down the West Coast were well aware of the Orange Express.

The season began with optimism at a peak. The Beavers had won twenty-six of thirty games in 1979–80 and had a strong nucleus returning. Included were six-foot-ten center Steve Johnson and athletic guards Blume and Mark Radford, all seniors. In addition, there were prize recruits Charlie Sitton, the highly sought star from nearby McMinnville High School, and Lester Conner, an all-around talent from Chabot Junior College in California.

Jim Anderson, Miller's top assistant, recruited the latter two and admittedly was concerned whether Conner would make it to Corvallis.

"Lester's high school coach had tipped me off about him," Anderson said. "Ralph even went to see him play, something he usually left to the assistants.

Steve Johnson helps cut down nets after Oregon State clinched the 1981 Pacific-Ten Conference championship. *Courtesy of OSU Athletics Media Relations.*

But Lester said he wouldn't come to a school whose head coach hadn't seen him play in person."

Finally, Conner set a day, long after the letter-of-intent signing period had opened, when coaches could come to the family home in Oakland and make final pitches. Anderson was there along with some head coaches, including Jerry Tarkanian of Nevada–Las Vegas. Miller and his wife, Jean, were on a family trip, and Anderson was uneasy about being the lone assistant coach in the bidding.

"That was shortly after the Mount St. Helens eruption [in Washington]," Anderson said. "Kind of playing a hunch, I put some ashes from the volcano in a bottle and took them to Lester's mother. She seemed to really appreciate that. Who knows, maybe it helped. Anyway, Lester decided to join us."

Conner arrived in Corvallis and immediately was warned by his new teammates of Miller's distaste for fancy passes and freelance play, things that had been an integral part of Conner's game when he led Chabot to a runner-up finish in the California Junior College Championship.

I happened to attend the pre-season practice the first time the Beavers had a full-court scrimmage. Miller was sitting on a folding chair at center court when, early in the scrimmage, Conner made a steal and raced down court, exchanging passes with Blume, on a two-on-one fast break. Finally, as he reached the top of the key, Conner whipped a behind-the-back pass to Blume for an easy layup.

Miller blew a whistle to stop play and beckoned for Conner to come to him. Sensing that he was about to be scolded, Conner approached and said, "Hey, Coach, it was a great pass."

Miller glared at him and said, "Lester, you don't know crap."

What Miller knew was that he had a superb talent in Conner. He just had to break him, much as a cowboy would do with a frisky stallion. Conner took the criticism the right way and shortly became a star on a team full of them.

Johnson, poised for a record-breaking season, probably understood the coach's confrontation with the newcomer better than anyone. After two years of frustration with the abrupt Miller's stinginess with praise, he came to understand and respect him. Years later, Johnson would say, "About the best compliment I got from Ralph was one day when he said, 'Well, you finally got that play right.' And that was it."

To those who didn't know him, Miller came across as gruff and unrelenting. He really wasn't. He just wasn't into patting players on the back, and he didn't want them ever to forget that he was the boss.

If Miller was particularly demanding on this team's players, I think it was because he recognized their potential. He finally had a roster that was virtually perfect for the fast-paced offense and pressing defense schemes he loved so much.

Conner, Blume and Radford were all quick and sticky defenders who were ready and willing to pick up opponents full court in Miller's two-two-one press. Johnson could run the court, too, and was there to initiate fast breaks.

Ralph Miller has a stern look as he instructs Lester Conner before sending him back into action in a 1981 game. *Photo by Mike Shields.*

Sitton, although a freshman, was ready to supply much-needed toughness inside. On top of that, OSU was loaded with fine perimeter shooters in Conner, Blume, Radford and Sitton, in addition to Rob Holbrook and Jeff Stoutt off the bench.

Looking back years later, Holbrook said, "If there had been a three-point line with that team, it would have been so sweet."

Miller also had gotten across the point that he had little tolerance for excessive dribbling, unnecessary bounce passes and dunk shots. I happened to bring up dunking to him one day. His grumbling response: "What do I think of dunk shots? I consider them an idiot's delight." He did, though, accept the no-frills dunks of Johnson off fast breaks.

Another time, Miller startled me with this observation: "The basket should be raised from ten to twelve feet for college and professional play. That won't happen, but it would make for a better game."

As the season unfolded, it became obvious that this team-oriented group had bought into their coach's philosophy completely, and the execution frequently had opponents struggling to avoid embarrassment. At times, the Beavers whipped the ball around the key like baseball infielders playing pepper. Making the extra pass to get a higher percentage shot became an integral part of their makeup.

"I can't even show them game films of themselves," Miller said. "All they do is clap. They are some bunch."

An early indication of the Beavers' passing prowess came in a 103–55 romp over Rhode Island at the Far West Classic in Portland's Memorial Coliseum. They had thirty-six assists on thirty-nine field goals, a mind-boggling statistic. It wasn't a fluke. They finished the season with assists on 69.2 percent of their field goals.

Field goal shooting? The Beavers, capitalizing on those extra passes, made 50 percent or more of their attempts in twenty-four of twenty-eight games. The topper was a school-record .725 percentage in a 78–61 rout of Oregon in the Ducks' McArthur Court.

Johnson was the ringleader, sinking 235 of 315 shots for a .746 percentage, a long-standing NCAA record. He was ten of ten against Oregon, twelve of fourteen against both Arizona and Stanford and fifteen of eighteen against Southern California. Despite frequently having foul problems, he averaged 21.04 points for the season.

Still, as a reminder that Johnson wasn't alone in this accuracy kick, Sitton sank all eleven of his shots while scoring twenty-three points in an 102–58 rout of Portland State.

When it came time to open Pacific-Ten Conference play, OSU couldn't have faced a tougher assignment: Arizona State at Tempe. This was a Sun Devils team with more than its share of NBA prospects, such players as Byron Scott, Lafayette "Fat" Lever, Sam Williams and Alton Lister.

It wasn't easy, but the Beavers led virtually all the way and won 71–67. The Orange Express then resumed crushing opponents and began a steady

Danny Evans (44) celebrates as a 1981 OSU win over UCLA is secured. Teammate William Brew (right) looks on. *Photo by Brent Wojahn/*Oregonian.

climb in the wire-service polls. The Beavers were number one in one poll and number two behind Virginia in the other when they traveled to Seattle to face a strong Washington team coached by veteran Marv Harshman. It looked for the longest time that night as if the bubble would burst.

The inspired Huskies, matching OSU's fast-paced game, took a 44–34 halftime lead, built the edge to twelve points early in the second half and still were in front by four inside the final thirty seconds. But the resilient Beavers wouldn't die. Holbrook took a pass from Conner and scored from the lane. Then Blume forced a game-saving jump ball, got the tip and Johnson hit a follow shot on Conner's missed jumper to force overtime. It was downhill from there as the Beavers won 97–91. Johnson was a monster with thirty-eight points on twelve of seventeen shooting and a perfect fourteen of fourteen on free throws.

Finally, with their record still perfect after twenty-two games, the Beavers became the consensus number one while relaxing at home on the day between games with the Washington schools. The coaches made plans to watch a Sunday TV game between Virginia, led by seven-foot-plus Ralph Sampson, and Notre Dame. I asked Miller if I could join them. "Sure, if you don't have anything better to do," he said.

Ralph Miller, not big on excessive celebrations, consents to a "low-five" with Lester Conner after another OSU win. *Photo by Brent Wojahn/*Oregonian.

The home of assistant coach Lanny Van Eman was the site for the viewing party, and Ralph sat in one corner watching quietly while his assistants and their wives cheered for the Irish. Momentarily, I got the idea that Miller really didn't care who won.

Inside the final thirty seconds, Virginia led 56–55, and Notre Dame called a timeout after a five-second violation call against the Cavaliers. Van Eman's wife, Jan, came through the room with a tray full of brownies. She offered one to Miller. "No thanks," he said. "I might throw up if they miss this shot." So, he did care.

Then he watched intently as the Irish's Orlando Woolridge missed a shot from the baseline, retrieved the ball in a scramble and swished an off-balance jumper that barely beat the final buzzer. Notre Dame had won 57–56, and that meant that the Orange Express would be alone on top of both wire-service polls.

There was celebrating around him, but Miller just leaned back in his chair, a satisfied smile telling a story of its own. Then he turned to Jan Van Eman and said, "Now I'll have one of those brownies."

I also was part of a humorous incident earlier when the Beavers were headed to Pullman to play Washington State. The team was scheduled to fly out of Portland International Airport to Spokane on a 2:30 p.m. flight the day before the game. Miller joined some of us media members in the lounge to socialize before takeoff. Aune was there, and so were Bud Withers (*Eugene Register-Guard*) and Bill Mulflur (*Oregon Journal*). As the flight time drew near, I twice mentioned to Miller that we should be going to the gate.

"Calm down, Robinson," he said, rolling his eyes. "Ropes [trainer Bill Robertson] will come and get us."

Robertson didn't, and we arrived at the gate just in time to see our plane taking off. Seemingly unperturbed, Miller collected everyone's tickets and handed them to me. "You're the rookie here," he said. "Go get us on the next flight." I had to admit it. This was a coach who had mastered the art of keeping his cool.

We got on a flight about an hour later, hopped into a rental car in Spokane and got Miller to Pullman just fifteen minutes late for his team's practice. Naturally, a few players who had been berated for tardiness in the past were eagerly awaiting his arrival.

As the regular season wound down, the highlights were an 89–63 thrashing of Washington in sold-out Gill Coliseum and a hard-earned 82–76 win over UCLA in the Bruins's Pauley Pavilion. It was OSU's first win over UCLA in Pauley in school history, and in a sign of the team's depth, Bill McShane, Johnson's backup, provided some key plays down the stretch.

An 80–62 home win over Arizona pushed the win total to twenty-six, and then came the deflating and unexpected finish, an 87–67 home loss to vengeful Arizona State and a late collapse against Kansas State in the NCAA tournament.

Against the Sun Devils, it was Parents' Weekend, and there was the pre-game introduction of player parents and what Miller described as "much hoopla." Johnson's wife, Janice, was there with the couple's one-year-old son, Marques. Blume took Marques in his arms at one point and paraded around the court holding the infant's right arm in the air with one finger extended. The crowd loved it.

As this was going on, I noticed Arizona State's starters standing with arms folded in front of them and major frowns on their faces. I took it as a bad omen for the Beavers, who already had clinched the Pac-Ten title with the win over Arizona. So I wasn't shocked that the Sun Devils won. The margin of victory was startling, though.

Looking on from sideline as Beavers score a victory are (left to right) William Brew, Ray Blume and Steve Johnson. *Photo by Brent Wojahn/*Oregonian.

Anyway, that took away the number one ranking, and the Beavers were headed back to Pauley Pavilion for the playoffs with a first-round bye. They expected to play San Francisco, but the Dons were upset by Kansas State in a first-round matchup.

Against the Wildcats, the Beavers immediately jumped in front, although they struggled at times with KSU's slow-paced offense. Still, OSU had a 26–19 halftime lead and went ahead 39–28 with 13:48 remaining. Typically, this would have been the time for the Beavers to go for the jugular. Surprisingly, they didn't.

Instead, they turned tentative and eventually crippled a Miller-ordered delay game in the final 7:00 by missing the front end of three one-and-one free throw opportunities. Suddenly, they found themselves in deep trouble. It didn't help when Johnson had a jump-hook basket waved off on a questionable offensive foul call. Finally, in an era without a shot clock, it was 48–48, and the Beavers were holding the ball for a final shot. Sitton was fouled with 2:03 left, and he missed the first free throw on the last of those crucial one-and-one chances.

The Wildcats rebounded and then set up for their own final field-goal attempt. It was no secret that Blackman, later an outstanding NBA player with the Dallas Mavericks, would take the shot, and Radford aggressively stuck to him. "I probably even fouled him a couple of times," Radford admitted.

With fifteen seconds showing, Blackman moved outside to get the ball. Then he worked his way to the baseline, Radford hassling him with constant pressure. A leaping Radford had an arm right in his face as he sank the game-winning eight-foot jumper with two seconds remaining, giving the Wildcats their lone lead of the game.

It was a dreadful way for the Orange Express to be derailed. I couldn't help but wonder if a season-earlier loss to Lamar in their playoff opener had something to do with the apparent apprehension.

After the game, Miller deftly handled interview questions, masterfully hiding his distress. A couple of days later, though, he admitted to me that he was having a difficult time getting over the season-ending defeat. Later, in his book *Ralph Miller: Spanning the Game*, written with Bud Withers (Sagamore Publishing, 1990), the Hall of Fame coach wrote that the Kansas State loss "will forever be one of my great disappointments."

The 1981–82 Beavers, led by Conner, Sitton and freshman A.C. Green, had better luck in the NCAA tournament, making it to the Elite Eight before losing to Georgetown 69–45. But that team was not as strong as its predecessor.

Miller, who was eighty-two when he died in 2001, truly believed that the 1980–81 Beavers were good enough to advance to the Final Four and make some noise there. I was among those who thought so, too.

# 9

# Legends in Their Own Time

I had an afternoon shift on that Monday in the fall of 1961, my second week in the *Oregonian* sports department. I was in a mellow mood and completely unprepared for what happened before I even had a chance to sit down at my desk.

"Robinson, get in here," an angry shout came from behind a partition at the opposite end of the office. Sports editor and columnist L.H. Gregory was beckoning to me, and obviously he wasn't in a congenial mood.

I entered his domain and took a seat next to a cluttered roll top desk that made you feel as if you had just gone back decades in a time warp. He looked up, squinted, removed a pipe from between his parched lips and asked, "Did you edit my Oregon State football story last Saturday?" I'm sure he already knew the answer, but I confirmed that I had been his "editor."

Those were the days when reporters on the road frequently sent their game stories via Western Union—to machines in our office—and I had been assigned to handle Greg's story. I'm sure I was selected for the assignment by a sports news editor who couldn't wait to observe my initiation.

"Now get this straight," Gregory said. "The only Beavers I mention in my stories or columns are the Portland Beavers [the city's Pacific Coast League baseball franchise]. You edited in several 'Beavers' in my story. Don't ever do that again."

I responded with a mild protest, pointing out that Oregon State and Beaverton High School also carried the Beavers nickname. He scoffed. "Doesn't matter. Just don't let it happen again." I didn't, and I soon became

L.H. Gregory, longtime sports columnist for the *Oregonian*, sits at a heavily littered roll top desk near the end of his career. *Courtesy of the* Oregonian.

aware that Orange or Orangemen were his chosen nicknames for Oregon State teams.

I also was fast coming to realize that I was working under a couple of prize members of what some have called sports' golden era—Gregory and Don McLeod, the executive sports editor and my immediate boss. They began their newspaper careers at a time when flowery writing was the rage and McLeod was a master of it. The writing style was about to undergo a gradual change, but at that time, quotes from coaches and players after games were a rarity in stories or columns of McLeod and Gregory.

McLeod also was a master practical joker, which I learned on my first day at the *Oregonian*. He assigned me to cover two games of the Women's World Softball Tournament, which was being played in Portland. He told me my deadline for the early edition was 5:00 p.m.

Unfortunately, at a few minutes before 5:00 p.m., the first game was still scoreless in the twentieth inning. I called the deskman and told him about the situation and that he wouldn't be getting an early-edition story from me. I could hear him relaying the news to McLeod, who asked to talk to me.

"What kind of a reporter are you?" he stormed, and I swallowed hard. "When I tell you to have a story in before a deadline, I expect to get it."

"But, Don," I said anxiously, "the game still is going. What do you expect me to do?"

For a moment, there was silence. Then I heard McLeod's laughter. "Had you going, didn't I?" he said.

Greg and Mac, as we called them, were some kind of pair, and some of the stories about them were priceless.

Gregory, who worked in the *Oregonian* sports department for fifty-two years before his retirement in 1973, was a stickler for grammar but wrote some of the longest and most confusing sentences and paragraphs imaginable in his "Greg's Gossip" column. Amazingly, though, those rambling sentences and paragraphs, if analyzed, were almost always grammatically correct.

His knack for coining nicknames for teams wasn't confined to Oregon State. There were the Tall Firs for the University of Oregon's 1939 national basketball champions and Black Tornado for then Medford High School (now North Medford). The Black Tornado nickname eventually was adopted by the school, replacing Tigers.

Johnny Pesky, the famed Boston Red Sox infielder and later coach, was from Portland and had his last name created by Gregory, who couldn't tolerate his real last name, Paveskovich.

I remember when electric typewriters became part of our operation. Classes were set up for instruction, and I happened to be in the same class with Greg. About twenty of us had been working for nearly an hour, learning the ropes, when Greg raised his hand and asked the instructor, "How do you turn this damn thing on?" Shortly thereafter, management gave the OK for Greg to continue to use his rickety manual typewriter with someone in the back shop processing his copy.

Gregory was sometimes cantankerous, oftentimes eccentric and usually aloof. Stone-set in his ways, he was a railroad buff, a student of the Civil War—the real one and not the one involving Oregon State and the University of Oregon. He hated to fly and would do some strange things to avoid traveling by plane. It was not unusual for him to drive from Portland to Los Angeles and back to cover a football game. He also was extremely superstitious. For instance, he didn't believe in paper money and usually was weighted down with pockets full of silver dollars.

McLeod's personality was much different, outgoing and fun loving. He had a keen vocabulary and loved to flaunt it. When a quarterback performed well, he would write that the quarterback had "tossed and bossed" his team to victory or that he had "donned the purple robes of gridiron royalty." My favorite of his creations was when he described Portland Buckaroos hockey goalie Don Head as "the padded guardian of the corded igloo."

There were times, too, when McLeod interviewed college coaches for advance stories on football or basketball games and left the coaches mystified by the words that he attributed to them.

McLeod, who began his career at the *Oregonian* in 1926 as a sportswriter, spent some time working in the newsroom before returning to the sports department as executive sports editor. He officially became sports editor when Gregory retired. It was while he was a news reporter that he came up with a series of scoops that prompted one of his superiors to call him "the finest crime reporter in the business."

He also became famed among his peers in 1937, when he sneaked on to an airplane and hid in a restroom until the plane was in flight from Portland to Southern California. Then he emerged and got his story about three Soviet fliers who were trying to complete a trans-Pacific flight from Moscow to San

Don McLeod, shown here in 1935, spent most of his career at the *Oregonian* as executive sports editor. *Courtesy of the* Oregonian.

Diego. Because of a need for fuel, the fliers landed in Portland, and that's when McLeod, rebuffed when he asked to interview the fliers, made his move.

Once settled into the sports department, McLeod became a first-class boss. Give him a solid effort and loyalty and he would do just about anything for you. Cross him and he never would forget it.

One of McLeod's best friends over the years was Harry Glickman, who once had been promised a sportswriting job at the *Oregonian* by McLeod upon his graduation from the University of Oregon. But when the time came, no job was available. So McLeod tried to get Tex Salkeld, a boxing promoter, to hire Glickman. When Salkeld balked, McLeod asked George Pasero from the city's other daily newspaper, the *Oregon Journal*, to help with the persuasion.

It worked. Glickman got the job and went on to become a highly successful Portland sports promoter, bringing NFL exhibition games to the Rose City along with minor-league hockey's Portland Buckaroos. Then he managed the successful bid to secure Portland an NBA franchise, the Trail Blazers.

But back to the stories about those sports media characters, Greg and Mac. Included would have to be the time when smoke nearly led to evacuation of the football press box at the University of California–Berkeley. Turns out that Gregory had not made sure that his pipe had been extinguished before putting it into a pocket of his trench coat.

Greg's trench coats were classics—always scruffy, dirty and with burn marks. Nick Bertram, a colleague of mine at the *Oregonian*, recalled an experience he had during a time when the newspaper was in the process of breaking a strike and had beefed up security in the building.

"I answered the phone one night, and it was Greg," Bertram said. "He was angry, and he told me to come down to the lobby because a guard wouldn't let him pass. I got down there and saw Greg slumped down in a wooden chair, wearing his trench coat and looking as if he had just come in off skid road. The guard said, 'Do you know this guy?' I told him that it was Greg, our sports editor. Greg jumped up, waved his arms and shouted, 'See, I told you so!' The next day the guard was gone."

It was before my arrival, but a couple of veteran staff members told me how Greg would recruit them to play catch with him with a baseball in the hall outside the office. Greg fancied himself as a pitcher, although the speed of his fastball would have made former knuckleball pitcher Tim Wakefield of the Boston Red Sox look like a fireballer.

Then there was the time that the Portland Beavers returned home from a road trip on a ten-game winning streak. Photographer Frank Sterrett, assigned to work the Beavers' first home game after their trip, asked Greg for a ride to the ballpark. When Sterrett opened the back door of Greg's car, he found the seat covered with peanut shells. He asked Greg about it.

"I started throwing the shells back there on the day the winning streak began," Greg explained. "It would be bad luck to take them out until the streak ends."

Sterrett couldn't resist after they arrived at the ballpark. As he took his camera from the back seat, he scooped out some of the shells. "Stop that," Gregory shouted as he ran around the car. Then he got down on his hands and knees to pick up shells and put them back into the car.

"He was a superstitious son of a gun," Sterrett said. "The Beavers lost that night, and Greg was mad at me for about three months."

And how about this one? Greg was in the office late one night to meet with a boxing promoter, getting information for a future column. When they were finished, the promoter asked Greg where he might go to get a bowl of chili at the late hour.

"You like chili?" Greg said. "Well, I'll take you to a place that serves the best chili in the state."

So the promoter hopped into Greg's car, and off they went. And went and went. There are conflicting stories of whether the destination was Pendleton, Bend or some truck stop in between. Suffice it to say that the promoter fell asleep, and when he woke up, it was going on daybreak.

Greg parked in front of an all-night diner and told his guest, "Here we are." Once inside, Greg ordered two bowls of chili and asked to talk to the chef. When the chef came to his table, Greg told him that he would like to have his chili recipe so it could be used in the food section of the *Oregonian*.

The chef seemed puzzled, then shrugged and returned to the kitchen. Moments later, he was back, holding an empty Dennison's can. "Open the can, pour the chili into a pan, put the pan on the stove and turn on the heat," he said.

If that's not exactly how it happened, it's close enough to make the point.

In the mid-1950s, Gregory still was pitching for the Oregonian Orioles, a media team that played some friendly baseball games with Oregon State and University of Oregon coaches. One year, at Oregon, the Orioles were short a player. So baseball coach Don Kirsch recruited Ducks All-American outfielder George Shaw to fill in on the media team. Shaw proceeded to make a couple of sensational catches to get Greg off the hook.

After the game, the gentlemanly Shaw came over and said, "Greg, you pitched a fine game." To which Greg replied, "Well, thank you, George. Did you see it?"

Don McLeod, as he looked shortly before retirement, had a flowery writing style and keen sense of humor as trademarks. *Courtesy of the* Oregonian.

As for that messy desk and the piles of books and papers that covered and surrounded it, many of us wondered if Gregory ever threw anything away. We perhaps got an answer when, after his retirement, Wayne Thompson was assigned to clean up the area of the desk. Among other things, he found a deep stack of papers covered with dust. On top was a press release from the University of Southern California, dated in 1926.

McLeod, who retired from full-time employment in 1978, liked to gamble, and the greyhound racing track was one of his favorite haunts, even after his retirement. He also was an astute poker player who was not above sending a cab to pick up a media patsy. "I paid for the cab, but I usually got my money back and then some," he said.

McLeod's racing connections weren't limited to Oregon, either. Bertram recalled a time when he and McLeod were in Phoenix, Arizona, on separate assignments.

"Mac asked me to go to the greyhound races with him," Bertram said. "We pulled up near the main office and out came two guys with a red carpet. They rolled it out from the door to our car. Then we were taken to a special box and wined and dined. The feature race that night was named after Mac, and after the race, he took me to the infield with him where he presented the owner of the winning dog with a blanket. It was an unreal experience."

Still, McLeod was at his entertaining best when he had the chance to hassle one of his reporters. Such an occasion came after a Saturday night when three of us, including the recently hired Jim Crowell, were about to close up shop at midnight. McLeod had told us that there might be a late call on a boxing tournament at the Warm Springs Reservation in Central Oregon, but it hadn't come.

Just as we started out the door, the phone rang, and Crowell, his coat in hand, answered. It was the call from Warm Springs, and he was stuck to take about fifteen minutes worth of results dictation. Disgusted, he kicked a foot in the air, and his loafer went flying through a large glass partition between the office and the hallway. Crowell was petrified about how McLeod would react.

Before Crowell arrived at work on Monday, McLeod had heard full details of the incident. "Watch this," he said, grinning, as he saw Crowell strolling down the hall toward our office. By the time Crowell walked through the door, McLeod was glaring in his direction. "Crowell, get over here," he said. Then, much as he had done with me on my first-day assignment, he made the trembling Crowell explain what had happened. Before Crowell could finish, though, McLeod broke into laughter and told him not to worry, that a janitor would be up soon to replace the glass. Then he winked at him and said, "Nice job on those boxing results."

In 1942, McLeod was headed to Los Angeles to cover an Oregon–Southern California football game. Before he left Portland, he got a call from a friend who was manager of the hotel where McLeod would be staying. The friend was seeking advice. He said he could get fourteen points if he took Oregon in a bet. McLeod told him to take the points because the Ducks had a good chance to win the game straight up.

"The Trojans won 40–0 and, when a cab brought me back to the hotel, I saw my bags on the sidewalk next to the front door," McLeod said. "As it turned out, my things still were in the room. Just the bags were outside. It all was in fun, but I got the message."

Gregory died in 1975, McLeod in 1989. But those who knew them well aren't likely to forget their legendary and seldom dull march through the sporting world of their time.

# 10

# Pericin and Showtime Hoops

It was halftime of one of his Portland State basketball team's games, and coach Marion Pericin was livid about the Vikings' first-half play.

"He was steaming," said Bob Grant, his assistant at the time. "He came storming into the locker room and let everyone know how he felt. He even slammed his fist into a chalkboard."

After calming down, Pericin talked to his players about what he expected of them in the second half. But when it came time for the Vikings to return to the court, he quietly called Grant aside.

"Bob, I think I broke my hand (on the chalkboard)," he said. "Would you take over up there? I'll be up as soon as I can."

About six minutes into the second half, Pericin returned to resume coaching. He had a towel with ice wrapped around his injured hand. Then he went about business as if nothing had happened.

While not his finest hour, this incident was a telling example of the passion Pericin had for the game, a passion that rubbed off on his players in his too-brief run at the PSU helm. Pericin coached the Vikings for only seven years, starting with the 1965–66 season. In that time, though, he turned the school's basketball program from a yawning afterthought into a high-octane attraction that produced a string of home sellouts in the small PSU Gym (later remodeled and renamed the Stott Center).

Pericin, a chatterbox on the sideline, was almost worth the price of admission by himself, jumping up and down, shouting instructions to his players, questioning calls by the officials, occasionally talking to fans. By the

Portland State basketball coach Marion Pericin joins cheering fans in a packed PSU Gym, later renamed the Stott Center. *Courtesy of PSU Athletics Media Relations.*

end of some games, he was so hoarse that he could barely communicate in post-game interviews.

"We want our games to be the most exciting in town," said Pericin, who came to Portland State after being a player and then an assistant coach under Hank Anderson at Gonzaga University.

In 1985–90, Paul Westhead gained fame for his run-and-gun teams at Loyola Marymount University. His Lions, in the process of winning twenty-three of twenty-eight games in the 1989–90 season, set an NCAA Division I record by averaging 122.4 points per game.

Pericin coached a similar style long before that but without funds to stock his roster with the kind of talent that Westhead had. In his tenure, the Vikings scored 100.0 or more points twenty-eight times, and in 1970–71, they averaged 99.2 points per game.

"Marion was well ahead of his time with his style," said Roy Love, the school's baseball coach at the time and later its athletic director. "I sometimes had the feeling that he would rather score one hundred points and lose than score seventy-five and win."

In addition to being fiery, Pericin was aggressive, enterprising and meticulous with his practices. He also had a tireless flair for entertainment and promotion. To the media, he was a much-appreciated quote machine—when he wasn't too hoarse to talk.

So as the Vikings advanced from the NAIA to the NCAA College Division to NCAA Division I under his watch, their popularity grew to the point that their gym, which seated fewer than two thousand, would be full and the doors locked for most games more than an hour before tipoff.

Spectators knew what to expect. The Vikings, relying on their zone presses, would check opponents full court and fast break at every opportunity. It was nothing for them to erase a ten-point deficit in two minutes or less.

Marion Pericin directs the team's high-octane offense from the sideline in a game late in his coaching career. *Courtesy of PSU Athletics Media Relations.*

In Pericin's second season, his team earned an at-large invitation to the College Division Western Regional. The draw was tough—against host San Diego State—and PSU lost 101–73 after scoring the game's first four points. The Vikings then lost to California-Davis 81–61 in a consolation game to finish the season with sixteen wins in twenty-five games. Hal Dohling, Bill Wilkerson, Peter Ness, Ed Gorman and Mike O'Gara were some of the members of that team.

"I don't think we were overmatched at San Diego," O'Gara said years later. "We just didn't get our game going, didn't play well."

The College Division caliber of play was impressive that season, and the national title was claimed by Winston-Salem (North Carolina), which featured future NBA great Earl Monroe. All the while, thanks to their coach, the Vikings provided all kinds of sidelight entertainment.

There was the night that Anderson brought his Gonzaga team to Portland, and as usual the gym was packed. But fans became restless as only the Bulldogs were on the court for pre-game warm-ups. Finally, the Vikings appeared, just in time for the national anthem and player introductions. Pericin had his players warm up in the building's secondary gym.

When Anderson had his school's pep band seated behind the Portland State bench for a game in Spokane, Pericin returned the favor in Portland.

In a game at the University of Puget Sound, Loggers students had small wooden blocks, which they clapped together in an effort to disrupt Pericin's talks to his team during timeouts. He grinned and ignored them at first, but when they began throwing the blocks in the direction of the PSU huddles, he held up the game and threatened to take his team off the floor. A public address announcement took care of the problem.

Then there were the victory cigars, an idea Pericin got from Red Auerbach of the Boston Celtics. When a win was secured, Pericin often would pull out a long cigar and stuff it into his mouth, unlighted, to the delight of his players and PSU fans.

The post-game parties, hosted by Pericin and his wife, Loretta (nickname Letty), in the family's Beaverton home, were classics. Friends, opposing coaches, school officials, media members and, sometimes, even the referees of that night's game were invited. Former PSU players often served as bartenders.

I once asked Pericin about the advisability of having referees involved in his parties. He laughed and said, "You never know. It might help us down the road."

Pericin's practices were extremely well organized, and he followed a strict timetable. Some joking and goofing off was allowed, but it was all business most of the time.

Tom Trebelhorn, who went on to a career in baseball managing and coaching, some of it in the Major Leagues, played basketball for Pericin for two years.

"I learned how to organize a practice calendar from Marion, not just day to day but for an entire season," Trebelhorn said. "I've used his philosophies ever since."

Trebelhorn said that Pericin was a "master at recruiting ordinary players—not particularly big or fast but with good attitudes. Then he would play to their strengths and get the most out of them."

Willie Stoudamire (right) races down court in a game against Idaho. He was a star on Marion Pericin's final Portland State team. *Courtesy of PSU Athletics Media Relations.*

As the years went by, Pericin pushed to improve his program. In 1969, he was among the leaders in supporting a move to put Portland State in NCAA Division I in all sports except football. He was convinced that his teams could have an immediate impact at that level.

Then came gradual disenchantment. He pushed without success for the kind of funding that would allow him to recruit higher-level players. He could see that, without more money for scholarships, his teams would lack the depth needed to compete with the big boys.

He also became frustrated with the NCAA, which insisted on an extended transition period before the Vikings would become eligible for national playoffs at their new level.

His later teams featured the Stoudamire brothers—Willie and Charlie—plus Leo Franz, Jerry Stephens and Craig West. He became particularly irked when Willie Stoudamire had a scoring average that would have placed him third in the nation in Division I for the 1971–72 season.

"But they wouldn't count our statistics," Pericin said. "Instead, they put our statistics in the College Division. But we no longer could play in the College Division tournament." He and his players felt like outcasts.

So after that 1971–72 season, Pericin decided to get out of coaching, leaving behind a PSU career record of 85-82, including 33-14 in his final two years. He worked for a shoe company, did some basketball camps, worked some games as a TV analyst and eventually became a marketing executive for Red Lion Inns. In the latter capacity, his specialty was luring visiting sports teams to stay at one of the Red Lion's Portland-area hotels.

Pericin, a popular sporting figure in the Portland area to the end, was sixty-five when he died in January of 1996. He left behind indelible memories of basketball without a speed limit.

# 11

# Maestro of the Giant Killers

It was absolute chaos in the Oregon State football locker room on that November day of 1967, and portly coach Dee Andros was milking the moment. Between back slaps and hugs, he kept an eye out for media members because he wanted them to hear what he was about to say to his jubilant players.

Finally, with the wildest of celebrations going on around him and OSU's Gill Coliseum seemingly shaking, Andros climbed onto a box and asked for silence. He raised his right-hand index finger above his head dramatically, hesitated for a moment and then shouted, "Who's number one now?" The bedlam just increased as players also raised index fingers in response to their leader. Tears trickled down Andros's cheeks as he continued.

"I told you fellows before the game that I thought you are the greatest bunch of kids who ever lived, and I still believe it," he said. Then the celebration continued. It was crazy, almost dangerous, in the overcrowded quarters.

The Beavers, already nicknamed the Giant Killers from earlier exploits, had just scored a historic 3–0 home win over top-ranked Southern California before a rain-dampened crowd of 41,494, the largest attendance for a sporting event in Oregon at the time. I was on hand that day as part of the *Oregonian* coverage team, and I marveled at the scene, a capper to an intense game featuring great defensive performances.

Down the hall, I found a subdued Trojans coach John McKay, and he paid tribute to the Beavers. "We performed well for most of the game," he said. "They just performed better." Asked if this was his toughest loss

Oregon State coach Dee Andros raises arms as a signal of the football upset of top-ranked Southern California in 1967. *Courtesy of OSU Athletics Media Relations.*

as USC coach, he replied, "This is the first loss that knocked us out of a national championship."

As the years have passed, I occasionally hear people talk of how the Beavers "stopped" Trojans star O.J. Simpson that day. In reality, that wasn't true. Simpson was kept out of the end zone, but he ran for 188 yards on thirty-three carries on the muddy field, hardly a subpar effort.

As it turned out, a thirty-yard field goal by Mike Haggard with a little more than five minutes left in the second quarter decided the outcome. Interestingly, the kick was almost the exact distance of an earlier missed field goal by the Trojans. OSU fullback Bill Enyart had a big day—135 yards on twenty-four carries—but the Beavers' resilient defense was what made the upset possible. I vividly recall one particular play, a tackle of Simpson from behind by Jess Lewis when Simpson was setting up his blockers near the sideline and appeared to be on his way to a touchdown.

Years later, Andros would look back and say, "You know, the whole game, I didn't think that field goal would hold up. The conditions didn't bother O.J. a bit. It just was a well-played defensive game by both teams."

I remember talking to OSU defensive lineman Ron Boley, who said, "He [Simpson] is the best we've faced, but he can have the Heisman Trophy. We'll settle for the win." Simpson didn't win the Heisman that year, but he did get it in 1968.

The Giant Killers nickname already was in place before the Trojans came to Corvallis because the Beavers had upset one second-ranked team (Purdue 22–14) and tied another number two (UCLA 16–16).

It was after the UCLA game that Andros made his fitting pronouncement: "I'm tired of playing these number two teams. Bring on number one."

Steve Preece, the Beavers' quarterback in 1967, chuckled as he recalled that Andros comment. "Dee also stalled around that day, making sure the writers were there, before he spoke."

Andros was kind of amazing with his knack for coming up with quotes that suited the media's needs. I always wondered how often his comments were spontaneous and how often pre-planning was involved.

As it turned out, the Beavers finished with seven wins, two losses and the tie with UCLA. They were edged out by USC for the Pacific-Eight Conference title, an early season loss to Washington and the tie costing them a trip to the Rose Bowl. Seventh-ranked in the final Associated Press poll, they got no post-season bid because of the conference rule at the time that only the champion was bowl eligible.

And McKay was wrong. The loss to the Beavers didn't keep the Trojans from a national championship, which they were awarded via wire-service polls after a 14–3 win over Indiana in the Rose Bowl.

As for Andros, affectionately nicknamed the "Great Pumpkin" early in his Oregon State career for his girth and the orange jackets that he so often wore, his coaching success went downhill dramatically not long after the Giant Killers season. Walking on the OSU campus one off-season day early in 1968, he happened to see one of his African American players, Fred Milton, sporting a beard and mustache. Andros had a strict rule against his players having facial hair.

"It wasn't as if I ran around looking for Milton," he said at the time. "But I saw him, and I couldn't let it pass."

Andros told Milton that he would have to remove the facial hair or be suspended from the team. He thought Milton was ready to comply. But Milton changed his mind at the encouragement of some activists on campus. Suddenly, it became a national civil rights issue with racial overtones. There were student protests and marches on campus, and the OSU Commission on Human Rights and Responsibilities ruled that Milton's rights had been violated.

I admired Andros for stubbornly refusing to budge under the pressure to adjust his program's rules. He knew he wasn't a racist and felt no need to prove it by changing his long-standing rules.

I'm sure the fact that he had been in tougher situations also was a factor in his stand. One of those times came when he was in the U.S. Marine Corps in World War II and was present as six soldiers raised the U.S. flag on Iwo Jima,

Dee Andros (far right) joins (from left to right) Oregon player Bobby Moore (later Ahmad Rashad), Ducks coach Jerry Frei and UO athletic director Len Casanova at a 1969 banquet. *Courtesy of the author.*

providing the world with a famous photograph. He also might have been influenced by his football play at Oklahoma under Bud Wilkinson, known as one of the game's most demanding disciplinarians.

It also wasn't lost on program insiders that Andros was on the conservative side as a disciplinarian in comparison with Tommy Prothro, his predecessor at the Beavers' helm.

Eventually, Andros weathered the storm as the OSU administration stuck with him and Milton transferred to Utah State. But the negative backlash from the Milton controversy dealt a major blow to his recruiting, especially of African American players. After winning seasons in 1968, 1969 and 1970, his last five teams won just thirteen of fifty-five games.

"It just was a different era, and Dee was one of those old-school coaches," Preece said. "He didn't want anyone dictating to him about his program. But believe me, if it had been me with the facial hair, he would have treated me the same way [that he treated Milton]. It had nothing to do with race. He was a phenomenal coach—one of a kind."

Hal Cowan, a former OSU sports information director, offered similar feelings. "It was a case of some non-athlete blacks using Fred and trying to make a fuss," he said. "Some people didn't like the image that Dee portrayed, but really, if you didn't like Dee, there was something wrong with you."

It was interesting, too, that Andros and Milton became very good friends later on. "It was so like Dee that he didn't hold a grudge," Preece said.

Many coaches wouldn't have survived the losing seasons that Andros endured. But the OSU administration stuck with him because of the positive results he gave the school in public relations and fundraising. Simply put, he was an ambassador dressed in orange who liked to refer to himself as the "Great Punkin," choosing his own pronunciation of his nickname. It didn't hurt, either, that his teams won nine of eleven games from archrival Oregon.

Eventually, he succeeded Jim Barratt as the school's athletic director from 1976 to 1985. He was inducted into the National Collegiate Directors of Athletics Hall of Fame, and he and the Giant Killers team also were inducted into the Oregon Sports Hall of Fame.

After his retirement, Andros continued to work as a special assistant for the Beaver Athletic Scholarship Fund. He was seventy-nine when he died in October of 2003 following a series of strokes and problems with diabetes.

Over the years, I got to know Andros even better while on my assignments on the golf beat. He often was a popular celebrity entry in pro-amateurs with his colorful personality. He was a lousy golfer but an engaging and sometimes riotous pro-am partner. He also was a shining light as an after-dinner speaker.

One time, he was talking to me about his thirty-six holes of play in a pro-amateur at Riverside Golf and Country Club in Portland. "The team used my score on one hole in two days," he said. "I made a short putt for a par on a par-three hole where the pro three-putted. So I played thirty-six holes and picked up my ball thirty-five times." He laughed and added, "I believe in perfection in everything except golf."

A club pro said of Andros's golf swing, "He has the flattest swing in golf, and it is absolutely necessary. Otherwise, he wouldn't have an unobstructed view [of the ball] over his stomach."

Andros's retort to that? "You know, any pro could learn from me. Just have him come out and play my second shots for a full round."

When a pro suggested that it might help his golf game if he lost sixty pounds, Andros said, "Hell, I can't do that. I'd spoil my image."

At a Pay Less Classic awards dinner one year at Riverside, Andros had actors Claude Akins and McLean Stevenson bent over in laughter when he said, "My football team had a two and nine record last season and that really upset my stomach. When my stomach is upset, I'm upset all over."

Jim Sweeney, the Washington State University coach for many of the years that Andros was coaching at Oregon State, combined with his friend for some great pro-am exchanges. One that I particularly enjoyed came at Riverside when Sweeney was playing the sixteenth hole while Andros was playing the par-five fifteenth, which has a pond in front of the green. A spectator waved to get Sweeney's attention and said, "Dee's in the water on fifteen." Sweeney shrugged and replied, "Don't worry, he'll float."

My favorite golf story involving Andros came at the Sunriver Resort in Central Oregon shortly after the Giant Killers season. The Oregon Sports Writers and Sportscasters Association was playing host to a tournament with college coaches and former players in the field. I was in charge of a special event the preceding day—a sole survivor competition with two-player teams using an alternate-shot format. One team would be eliminated on each hole until a winning twosome was determined.

I carefully paired the teams to provide parity. Andros came in with the highest handicap of twenty-seven. So I partnered him with the lowest-handicapped player in the field—former OSU basketball star Jim Jarvis, with a three. Andros was fired up. He rented a cart and hit some balls on the driving range. He was convinced that Jarvis would carry him deep into the competition and perhaps to victory.

The first hole that we played on the resort's Meadows course (since remodeled) was a shortish par five with a water hazard behind an elevated green.

"I'll hit the first tee shot for us," Jarvis told Andros. "That will put the ball out there where you can get it close to the green [with the second shot]."

Then Andros watched in shock as Jarvis cold-topped his drive, the ball going barely seventy-five yards. Andros followed with perhaps the best three-wood shot of his life. Jarvis figured his nine-iron was just right for the next shot, but the ball carried over the green and into the hazard. After a penalty drop, Andros hit a fine pitch shot to within seven feet of the cup. But Jarvis missed the putt. The team had made a double-bogey and was the first one eliminated.

"Damn, Jarvis, I thought you were a good golfer," Andros grumbled as his embarrassed partner climbed into the cart beside him.

The amusing sight of Andros driving that cart back to the clubhouse with Jarvis slumped next to him is indelible in my memory bank. It must have been one of resort's shortest-ever cart rentals.

# 12
# Marking Time with Mark All

Mark All looked at me warily. He backed away, seemingly watching my every move.

"Just give him time," said Ralph Long. "He'll come around."

It was a brisk August morning of 1963. I was at the kennel of Dock Shockley to do a story for the *Oregonian* on a day in the life of a racing greyhound. Long was Shockley's trainer, and Mark All was a star of the Multnomah Kennel Club's season at nearby Fairview Park.

I had picked Mark All for this story because, at a little more than two and a half years of age, his record was show-stopping. He had won six consecutive races and would be going for number seven that night at the track east of Portland, near Wood Village. Naturally, he would be an overwhelming betting favorite.

It was shortly before 9:00 a.m., and Long explained that Mark All, along with Shockley's other dogs, had been taken from the kennel at 6:45 a.m. for a romp in an exercise pen. He was back in the kennel by 8:00 a.m. for rest, and now it was time for a comb-and-brush session and then another trip to the exercise pen. I watched the grooming from close up. Then, on the way to the exercise pen, I noticed that Mark All seemed to have accepted that I was an OK guy. He playfully sidled up to me and allowed me to pat him on the head.

"It is a misconception that greyhounds are mean," Long said. "They're really quite friendly and playful. Most of them love children."

We returned to the kennel at 11:00 a.m., and Long informed me that Mark All would be staying there until dinnertime at 4:00 p.m. His quarters seemed nice enough—a mattress of shredded paper that obviously was changed frequently for cleanliness. He seemed happy as he settled in.

Long then gave me a bit of history about Mark All. He had been born in December of 1960 from the father-mother combination of Sunmarker and Lady All. As with all Long-trained greyhounds, he had been run through a strenuous training program as a pup, capped by a session in Kansas, where he had spent two weeks chasing jackrabbits (a practice made illegal not long after my visitation day). Then came a series of schooling races with the artificial lure, first without a starting box and then with the box.

At the tender age of eighteen months, Mark All was ready for the racing wars. His first race had been at Fairview Park the previous summer, but he had run at other tracks nationwide since with mostly outstanding results.

After a lunch break and some time on other newspaper duties, I returned to the kennel. Long greeted me, and as dinnertime approached, he described the meal schedule.

"We feed our dogs only once a day except on days when they are racing," he said. "The daily meal consists of horse meat, spinach, mackerel, Karo syrup, all-bran and vitamins. The ingredients are mixed in a large tub, and each greyhound is fed a different portion depending on the dog's weight."

Then Long explained that Mark All's dinner menu was different on days when he was racing. Instead of a full meal at 4:00 p.m., he would get only a small ball of horse meat soaked in syrup. His major feeding would come after his return from the track later that night.

Greyhound races, such as this one, were highly popular at the track east of Portland in the 1980s. *Courtesy of National Greyhound Racing Association.*

Of course, when the dog gets the smaller portion of the syrup-flavored horse meat, he immediately knows that he is going to be racing that night. In Mark All's case, there was a sudden personality change with the realization. His muscles tensed, and he looked stressed and uncomfortable.

"He's always obedient except after he realizes he is going to be racing," Long said. "He'll be hard to control then, and when we get to the track, he won't even listen to me. I think the major difference between the top racing dogs and the also-rans is this tenseness just before a race. Mark All surely has it."

Later, as race time approached, Mark All seemed to be a nervous wreck. Long assured me it was not unusual, simply the way that many of the dogs react when the challenge of a race draws near.

Fifteen minutes before post time, I left Mark All and the upcoming race's waiting area to place a modest bet to win on my new greyhound friend. The payoff wouldn't be huge, but that was all right.

Finally, it was time for Mark All to enter the starting boxes with eight sleek rivals. There were whining sounds and a lot of barking. Then the artificial "rabbit" began its electronic run, and the boxes were opened. Out came Mark All and the others with a furious rush.

Modern greyhound racing, an offshoot of coursing from an earlier time, had its beginning in the United States after Owen Patrick Smith perfected an artificial lure system in Hot Springs, South Dakota, early in the twentieth century. The first track was opened in Emoryville, California, in 1919.

"That first track wasn't too successful," said Gary Guccione, executive director of the National Greyhound Racing Association. "The sport really didn't take off until track operators in Florida went to night racing to avoid competition with horse racing."

One of the earliest tracks in Florida—Derby Lane in St. Petersburg—still is in operation and can claim the sport's longest history in the United States.

By the mid-1920s, there were tracks all over the country. Portland entered the picture in 1933, when founder Murray Kemp created Multnomah Kennel Club with races held at Multnomah Stadium (now Jeld-Wen Field). In 1956, because of a move of Portland's Pacific Coast League baseball franchise to Multnomah Stadium, the dog races were relocated to Portland Meadows, a horse racing facility. They were there for just one year before another move in 1957 to the ninety-acre site near Wood Village.

The new track/stadium was named Fairview Park initially and then renamed Murray Kemp Greyhound Park in honor of the founder. In 1991, the name was changed again—to Multnomah Greyhound Park.

The Oregon facility had its most successful run in the 1980s with a record attendance of 611,430 in 1987. Then came an attendance decline in the 1990s along with some shifts in ownership. Eventually, the operation was sold to Magna Entertainment, which also controlled Portland Meadows.

When it became obvious that the dog and horse operations couldn't coexist and be successful, the greyhound park was closed in December of 2004. It appeared briefly in 2012 that the property might become the site of a privately funded casino complex, but voters squelched the proposal.

Still, greyhound racing nationwide has survived through tough competitive and economic times, and twenty-three tracks remained in operation through 2012. Guccione is proud, too, that the myth of greyhounds being poor pets has been stifled for the most part, virtually eliminating the early trend of putting dogs to sleep after their racing days if they weren't in demand for breeding.

"There are about 150,000 greyhounds out there right now that have become pets," he said.

Guccione also perked up when he heard the identity of the greyhound I had featured in my long-ago story. "Oh, yes, I remember Mark All, a fine dog," he said. "I was in high school at the time and I saw him run [at the Wood Village track] a couple of times."

Now back to that night in 1963 and Mark All's bid for a seventh consecutive victory. He was in the middle of track and seemingly ready to charge into the lead as the field reached the first turn, commonly referred to as the escape turn because jostling so often went on there.

Suddenly, a dog from the inside bumped into Mark All and knocked him off stride and to the outside. In an instant, he was left in the dust. He did well to rally and finish sixth. I couldn't help but be amused by my bad racing luck. I pulled the betting stub from my pocket and discarded it in a nearby garbage can. My story had an ending that I hadn't anticipated.

I still occasionally think about Mark All and that day I spent with him. It was a good day, an interesting and educational one. As for the race and my bet, I just happened to have had the right dog on the wrong night.

# 13

# The Day After the Storm

Terry Baker recalls leaving Gill Coliseum in Corvallis on that overcast Friday afternoon. He had just finished a meal with his Oregon State University football teammates and was looking ahead to a big game the next day against the University of Washington in Portland's Multnomah Stadium. The date was October 12, 1962.

"I noticed that the wind was blowing pretty hard," he said. "But there were no big trees around the Coliseum to give me a clue as to what was happening, so I didn't think much about it."

It wasn't long after that, though, that Baker, a versatile quarterback who would go on to win the Heisman Trophy as the college game's best player for that season and to be featured as *Sports Illustrated*'s Sportsman of the Year, learned differently. That strong wind that he described was actually part of arguably the most intense storm to hit the Pacific Northwest since a crippling snowstorm on January 9, 1880. That one frequently has been referred to as the "Great Gale."

What became known as the Columbus Day Storm attacked with little warning. Weather forecasters hadn't seen it coming, reporting only that the day would be windy. So I was among those caught unaware.

I happened to be speaking to a group of budding high school journalists at the University of Oregon when the storm hit. It was early in my sportswriting career at the *Oregonian*, and I thought I had prepared a talk that the group of about thirty would enjoy. We were in a building a short way from the School of Journalism building.

I had barely begun my presentation when I noticed that seemingly no one was paying attention. Instead, the students were looking out windows and whispering to one another. It was as if I weren't even there.

Puzzled and annoyed by the lack of attention, I finally paused and said, "Am I really that boring?"

Terry Baker passed for two touchdowns, but Oregon State lost to Washington 14–13 in 1962 on the day after the Columbus Day Storm. *Courtesy of OSU Athletics Media Relations.*

"It's not that, Mr. Robinson," one of the female students said. "I think you should look out the window."

What I saw was shocking. Three mammoth trees had been blown over near the building. Debris of all sorts was swirling about. Startled college students were scurrying in all directions on a campus that suddenly was beginning to look like a battlefield. So much for my presentation. I hurriedly guided my group back to the School of Journalism, all of us battling to keep the wind from blowing us off balance. Then I departed to check on my car. I had parked it on a side street within a few feet of a large maple tree.

I was lucky. The maple tree had been blown down, but it had fallen parallel to my car and not on top of it. Later, as darkness approached and the wind had died down some, I made the Eugene-to-Portland drive home, proceeding slowly and dodging limbs and other debris on the highway.

The storm was classified as an extra tropical cyclone. Winds gusted to more than one hundred miles per hour at its peak. One gust on Portland's Morrison Street Bridge was measured at 116 miles per hour.

Damage was devastating. Thousands of trees went down in Oregon, some falling onto nearby buildings and cars. Shingles were scattered everywhere, and undamaged homes were the exception. Farm animals were crushed by collapsing structures. High-voltage transmission towers toppled. Radio and television broadcasting and telephone service were interrupted. Power outages were extensive, and electricity was not restored for several weeks in some areas.

Amazingly, though, it was decided that the OSU-Washington football game would go on as scheduled when Saturday turned out to be a clear, sunny day with virtually no wind. The Beavers traveled to Portland on buses that morning. It was a stark contrast to a day earlier when the storm's fury had brought cancellations or postponements of just about all activities, including all but a couple of downstate games on a large high school football schedule.

Still, it took yeoman efforts by many to get the stadium (now called Jeld-Wen Field) ready. Large portions of the stadium roof had been blown away. Seats had been damaged by falling debris and were replaced by portable chairs. Crews began work early in the morning and were busy clearing debris from the stands and the rain-softened playing field right up until game time. Electricity was out for most of the stadium, including the scoreboard, and also for the adjoining Multnomah Athletic Club, where the teams dressed in candlelight.

I was part of the *Oregonian*'s coverage team and, with the elevator out of commission, was among media members who reached the press box via a stairway that some of us didn't know existed.

Amazingly, a crowd of 30,030 showed up to watch the Huskies and Beavers, both high-quality teams with bowl-game aspirations, renew their rivalry. I always have felt that many of those attending simply used the outing as an escape from the frustrating mess that the storm had left in its wake.

Despite soggy field conditions, the game turned out to be a down-to-the-wire gem. Washington finally prevailed 14–13, the victory margin provided by a missed extra-point opportunity by the Beavers.

Terry Baker, a threat running and passing for Oregon State, poses with awards after winning the 1962 Heisman Trophy. *Courtesy of OSU Athletics Media Relations.*

OSU, which got scoring passes of six and ten yards from Baker to Vern Burke, led 13–7 before the Huskies drove to the game-winning touchdown with just over two minutes remaining. Charlie Mitchell got it on a two-yard run. Junior Coffey had run forty-three yards for the other Washington touchdown.

"It was a really tough loss for us," Baker recalled. "We didn't know it at the time, but later, Coach [Tommy] Prothro told us it probably cost us a chance to play in the Orange Bowl."

Oregon State and the University of Oregon were playing as independents at the time, and the Beavers went on to play in the Liberty Bowl, the game in which the left-handed Baker made a historic ninety-nine-yard end sweep for a touchdown in a 6–0 win over Villanova. They finished the season with a record of nine wins and two losses.

The Huskies, then playing in the Association of Western Universities, concluded their season with seven wins, one loss and two ties. They missed out on a Rose Bowl bid by losing to Southern California 14–0. The Trojans went on to edge Wisconsin 42–37 in the Pasadena classic.

Interestingly, Baker also encountered problems with the weather—a frozen field—at the Liberty Bowl in Philadelphia.

"I think the fact that we wore tennis shoes gave us an edge because of the better footing we had with them," he said. "The Villanova players seemed to slip more than we did. On my long run, two players almost had me in the end zone [for a safety] but missed, probably because of the slippery surface. When I got to the outside, I was wide open."

Baker chuckled as he recounted how the late Prothro repeatedly told people that Baker had called the play that resulted in his long touchdown run. "Really, it wasn't a smart play to call from that field position," he said. "If I did call it, I honestly don't remember doing it."

As for the post-game scene on that day at Multnomah Stadium, it was bizarre and provided me with sidebar material that was anything but routine. For instance, because of the power outage, there was no hot water for showers in the Multnomah Athletic Club. I remember cringing at the shrieks of players showering in cold water.

Now, looking back, Baker recalled going with some teammates to a friend's home in nearby Lake Oswego after that game and coming to realize just what the Columbus Day Storm was all about.

"The house where we went was next to the lake, and I remember that it took us a long time to get there," he said. "It was a hard-to-believe scene, like driving through a war zone."

14

# A Long-Overdue Payback

Jack Nicklaus was chatting with his Portland Open pro-amateur partners as they waited at the first tee for the fairway to clear. In a matter of minutes, they would be starting their round at Columbia Edgewater Country Club on that fall day of 1963. Approximately two thousand spectators were packed around the tee, eager to watch Nicklaus, golf's latest phenom and the tournament's defending champion, in action.

At the same time, another pro-am foursome was coming up the adjoining eighteenth fairway with only a few stragglers as a gallery. I was in that group and had not the slightest inkling that I was about to experience my most embarrassing moment as a sportswriter. It turned out to be a whopper and would come courtesy of Barney Keep, a well-known radio personality of the time.

Keep later admitted that it was a spur-of-the-moment idea, which made it the type of spontaneous reaction that had earned him such a following on the airways. I wasn't lucky enough to have it come in a press box, or a coach's office or a steamy locker room. Instead, it had to happen in an extremely public setting—at the pristine golf club located barely a pitching wedge distance from the banks of the historic Columbia River.

For background, Keep went to Oregon State (then called Oregon State College) to study forestry. He played on the freshman football team under Hal Moe and, among his activities, took an interest in radio. As a student, he got his start at station KOAC in Corvallis and soon showed that he was a natural with his humorous, off-the-wall style.

Barney Keep (left) has businessman Bob Hazen among his admirers at his ceremonial final radio show on KEX in 1979. *Courtesy of the* Oregonian.

Keep earned his degree in forestry in 1942 but was destined for a radio career. By 1944, he had his own *Morning Show* on KEX in Portland. The show earned him almost instant popularity and became a daily laugh fest for listeners. It had amazing staying power, continuing for thirty-five years before Keep, often referred to as "Lovable Ol' Barn," retired on Valentine's Day of 1979.

Keep's final show was broadcast from Portland's Civic Auditorium, and there were no empty seats. There was little doubt that he had been Portland's best-known radio personality of his era.

One-liners seemed to pour out in Keep's baritone voice, quickly and incisively. He was a master of the ad-lib, and the world was his target. He took particular delight in turning politicians into his personal punching bags. When he died at eighty-three in July 2000, Norm Maves Jr. of the *Oregonian* wrote, "He made his listeners wince, squirm and hide with his understated needle."

He once told a journalist, "When I go, what I want on my stone is 'Barney Keep. He made somebody laugh one time.'" He also got away for years with affectionately referring to wife, Eleanor, as the "Biscuit Burner" on the air.

Keep also frequently was part of his city's sporting scene. He was a good bowler and a fair-to-middling golfer who often played at the Eastmoreland municipal course. Those were the circumstances that brought us together for that Portland Open pro-amateur.

Gene "Bunny" Mason, the CE head pro, invited Keep, KGW-TV sports anchor Doug LaMear and me to play with him as a media group. We would be given a chance for a preview look at the tournament course and would not be part of the competition. I was delighted with the opportunity.

Mason, a noted quipster himself, and Keep made the round anything but serious. I'm sure players in nearby foursomes heard the frequent outbursts of laughter emanating from our group and wondered about our sanity.

Anyway, when we got to the par-four eighteenth hole—the ninth hole of the club's outside nine—I hit a typical short drive. Not so typically, the ball ended up in the middle of the fairway. That's when I noticed the large gathering of spectators around the first tee, within a few yards of the eighteenth green. I could see Nicklaus and his golden blond hair in the distance, too.

As I prepared for my second shot with a fairway wood, I thought to myself, "Aim to the left side of the green. Whatever you do, don't hit the ball to the right and into those spectators." Then, naturally, I sliced the shot into rough within a few feet of the spectators and behind a large bunker. I approached my ball, grateful that I hadn't hit anyone with my errant shot. I wanted to make my next shot quickly, before too many people noticed my predicament.

But just as I was taking my pitching wedge out of the bag, Keep's booming voice rang out loud and clear: "Ladies and gentleman, about to hit this difficult shot over the bunker is the Egyptian Open champion, Bob Robinson."

Suddenly, spectators turned away from the first tee and were virtually surrounding me. I was new on the golf beat, so I doubt that many of them knew me. I heard one fellow say, "I didn't know the Egyptian Open champion was playing here." I think he was serious.

Meanwhile, Keep, LaMear and Mason were on the green and enjoying the show. I momentarily stared at Keep with my best look of annoyance. His devilish grin was anything but sympathetic.

Suddenly, my hands were quivering and my throat was dry. I'm sure my pulse was double its normal rate. I tried deep breathing in an effort to relax. It didn't help much. Then, as I took my stance, I saw some movement out of the corner of my right eye. I looked up, and there, not more than ten feet away, stood Nicklaus, his arms folded in front of him and looking very much amused.

I would like to report that I hit a fine shot over the bunker and close to the cup. I didn't. Instead, I skulled the shot into the sand, prompting some muffled laughter from spectators. By the time I had pulled out my sand wedge, Nicklaus was back at the first tee, and most of the spectators had turned away. My humiliation was complete.

After we finished the round, I laughed along with my three pro-am partners about my experience, but it was an act. The embarrassment still was burning me. At one point, I told Keep, "Someday, somehow, I'm going to get even with you." He offered a smile that seemed to say, "Good luck with that."

Interestingly, Nicklaus never brought up my skulled shot in times we conversed that week and over the years. What a gentleman!

Now fast-forward to 1971 when some male amateur golfers complained to me that female golfers played too slowly. I wrote about their opinions. Several women reacted by insisting that it was not so, that women actually played faster than men.

I decided to do some research at that year's Portland City Best-ball tournament at the Rose City municipal course. Both the men and women played in foursomes on different days, and I randomly timed various groups and found that, on the average, the women finished their rounds about ten minutes faster than the men.

With that information duly reported, I planned to do a follow-up column on women's pet peeves with male golfers. I got some good responses.

"They give too many putts. They hardly ever putt out, and after all, that's part of the game," Ruth Varney said.

"Men can't help but play slower than women. They spend all of their time needling each other and worrying about the women playing up ahead," Molly Cronin told me.

"It takes men ten to fifteen minutes on the first tee just to decide for what they are going to play. Then, a few holes later, they start pressing and coughing [their bets], and more time is wasted," Maude Borst said.

"Men keep talking about past holes [they have played] over and over until you wonder if they can talk about anything else," Mildred Mitchell added.

Finally, out of the blue, came this comment from Mary Jossi: "The worst thing that can happen to you is to play in the group in front of that rude Barney Keep because he will hit [his ball] into you."

Jossi looked puzzled at my smile of joy. She would find out soon enough the reason for it.

Anyway, I wrote the column and gave prominent mention to Jossi's pet peeve. Then I waited patiently for the phone call that I figured would come. It did, the day after the column appeared.

I answered, and there was momentary silence on the line. Finally, without needing to identify himself, Keep said, "You got your payback, didn't you?" I said, "Yep, but I'm sorry it took the Egyptian Open champion so long." Then we both laughed.

One of Keep's endearing qualities was that he could take it just as well as he could dish it out.

# 15

# Big Mac in a Big Way

Mac Wilkins remembers vividly the Sunday afternoon practice sessions in his freshman year at the University of Oregon. He would go to Hayward Field at about noon, warm up and then wait patiently for the arrival of Ducks coach Bill Bowerman.

"Bill and his wife, Barbara, would come to the field after attending church," Wilkins said. "Then Barbara would sit in the stands and read a book while Bill worked with me."

The interesting twist to this story is that the work was with the javelin and not the discus, the event in which Wilkins eventually broke world records and won a gold medal at the 1976 Olympic Games.

"Really, at that point, I thought the javelin was my most natural event," Wilkins said. "But I just hadn't had enough experience with it. That's why we were having those Sunday sessions."

Wilkins attended Clover Park High School in Washington through his junior year, and the javelin was not part of the track and field program there. So Wilkins competed first in the shot put and then the discus and also ran some hurdles races. "Believe it or not, when I was in the ninth grade, my ambition was to be a miler and run for Bowerman," he said. "That goal didn't last long."

He took up the javelin as a senior at Oregon's Beaverton High School in 1968 and threw 195 feet the first time he competed. He thought he was on his way. He threw 225 feet in the summer before his freshman year at Oregon and had a 240-foot throw as a freshman after his Sunday workouts with Bowerman.

Mac Wilkins prepares for a discus throw in 1976 when he broke world record four times before winning an Olympics gold medal. *Photo from Mac Wilkins collection.*

"But my lack of experience caught up with me," Wilkins said. "The javelin is a violent event that makes you susceptible to injury if you don't know exactly what you are doing."

His injury came to his right elbow, probably because he just pushed himself too hard. The pain lingered and eventually forced him to abandon the javelin and turn his concentration back to the discus and shot put.

"What I needed was Tommy John surgery," Wilkins said. "But that procedure wasn't yet an option. I'll always wonder what might have been if that surgery had been available to me at the time."

The surgery, first performed by Dr. Frank Jobe in 1974, was named after John, a Los Angeles Dodgers pitcher, because he was the first to undergo it. Involved was a graft procedure called ulnar collateral reconstruction in which a ligament in the elbow was replaced by a tendon from another part of the body. It was considered no better than a long shot to help him.

But the procedure worked out well, and John was able to resume his major-league career. Later, the procedure became more common for athletes, especially baseball pitchers.

Anyway, Wilkins went on to major success in the discus and shot put, especially the former. As a UO junior, he placed fourth in the discus at the 1972 NCAA Championships. Then he won the discus title the following year.

I first did extensive coverage of Wilkins, whose father, Dick, had played on Oregon's 1949 Cotton Bowl football team, at the 1976 U.S. Olympic Trials in Eugene. He already was well known worldwide because of performances earlier that year.

His surge into the spotlight began in April when he broke John Powell's world record in the discus with a throw of 226 feet, 11½ inches at the Mount Sac Relays in California. Then, in a meet at San Jose State in May, he pulled off a most amazing feat. He broke the world record on each of three consecutive throws: 229; 230, 5½; 232, 6.

"I made adjustments on each of those throws, too," Wilkins said. My curiosity demanded that I ask him why adjustments were necessary after world-record throws. He replied, "You always are seeking the perfect throw. You know there is no such thing as a perfect throw, but you still seek it."

When Wilkins came back home to Hayward Field to begin his quest for a gold medal, he was a sight to behold. He was 250 pounds of bulging muscles and wore his hair long. He also sported a beard and mustache. He was a mean-looking dude with a swagger of self-confidence. Needing only to place among the top three to earn a trip to the Games in Montreal, he later admitted that he wasn't even trying to peak for the Trials.

Powell also was there and engaged in amusing exchanges of hyperbole with Wilkins. "John and I had a sometimes friendly rivalry," said Wilkins, who spent considerable time training with Powell in San Jose. "It took me awhile to get used to John and keep from getting irritated at him."

If Powell was trying to distract Wilkins, he failed, but his efforts were entertaining. After the discus prelims, he said, "Sure, it surprised me when Mac started to pop those big throws [in April and May]. In a way, I saw the potential early in the year when he put the shot over sixty-eight feet. I just hoped it wouldn't carry over to the discus. Now I watch the photographers take pictures of him. I wish I had a camera. I would take some pictures of him myself."

In between the prelims and the finals, Powell made some other tongue-in-cheek remarks. "When I look at Wilkins's raw potential, I'm honored just to

Arms folded, Mac Wilkins waits for the start of the discus competition in the 1976 U.S. Olympic Trials in Eugene. *Photo from Mac Wilkins collection.*

be in the same discus area with him," he said. "I probably have had my best year ever and nobody noticed because of Mac."

Finally, tired of the jesting, Wilkins said, "A year ago, I was sitting with John [at a meet], and he told me that it takes time to learn the discus. He said I was a rookie." Then Wilkins laughed and added, "How much time does it take to go from a world record to being just another discus thrower?"

Later, Wilkins talked about how he and Powell often played tennis and table tennis in breaks from their training in San Jose. "John was very good at table tennis," he said. "I would win about once in every twenty games."

Wilkins won the Trials discus with a throw of 224, 2. "My timing was off [in the finals]," he said. "I should have thrown farther." Powell finished second and Jay Silvester third.

In a way, Wilkins's performance at the Trials gave a mental lift to die-hard Eugene track and field fans who still were somber over the 1975 death of popular distance runner Steve Prefontaine in an automobile accident.

Looking back, Wilkins said, "I knew Pre about as well as anyone, but I wasn't there [at the Trials] for Pre. I was there for me. All of my concentration was on that."

At Montreal, Wilkins threw 224 feet in the prelims, an Olympic record at the time. Then he claimed his gold medal with a toss of 221, 5 in the finals. East Germany's Wolfgang Schmidt was second.

Wilkins added to his fame by winning a gold medal at the Pan American Games in San Juan, Puerto Rico, in 1979 and a silver medal at the Olympic Games in Los Angeles in 1984. A chance for another Olympics gold medal was lost when the United States boycotted the 1980 Games in Moscow at a time when Wilkins was in his prime.

Mac Wilkins, thirty pounds lighter and with hair trimmed shorter, has a much different look in 2010. *Photo from Mac Wilkins collection.*

"I might have gone in as the favorite at Moscow, but I don't know if I could have won," he said. "There was a lot of talk about questionable measurements and other homer tactics over there. It didn't seem like an accident that Russians won all of the throwing events."

Wilkins's world record was broken by Schmidt in 1980.

He was in Iceland for a meet and was getting ready for the competition when he got the news of Schmidt's record.

"I almost got the record right back that day," he said. "I threw a good one, but it was out of the sector [and didn't count]. The discus actually landed in the middle of the track." Because of the throw's length, it was measured anyway out of curiosity. "Approximately 238 feet," Wilkins said.

Also in 1980, Wilkins pushed his discus personal record to 232, 10½ at a meet in Helsinki, Finland. His other personal records were: shotput (69, 1¼), javelin (257, 4) and hammer (208, 10).

I found it interesting that, by the time he retired from competition, Wilkins had definite thoughts about what he eventually wanted to do: coach throwers. First, though, he worked in technology sales in Seattle for eight years (1990–98) before deciding it was time to create a career that would be less lucrative but would give him the satisfaction that he coveted.

"I began going to [track and field] meets and passing out fliers about throwing camps," he said.

He had some success with the camps, and that eventually led to his hiring in 2005 as a throws coach at Concordia University in Portland. He made it clear before taking the job that he had no designs on becoming a college head coach. He was down to 220 pounds. His hair was cut much shorter, and most of the facial hair was gone.

Then, in the fall of 2008, he opened the Mac Wilkins Throwing Academy in northeast Portland. Concordia throwers use it, but it is available for others, too, in regularly scheduled sessions or spur-of-the-moment arrangements. Wilkins also worked periodically at a track and field training center in Geneva, Ohio.

"Coaching throwers simply is my passion," he said. "It has been for a long time."

When the 2012 U.S. Olympic Trials returned to Hayward Field, Wilkins did some work as a TV analyst for Comcast Sports Northwest. In that role, he had a downright scholarly look about him. It was quite a contrast from the self-described "wild look" that he had back in 1976.

# 16

# LPGA: Behind the Scenes

Many fine athletes have played on the LPGA Tour over the years, quite a few after major accomplishments in other sports. None has seemed more interesting to me than Japan's Ayako Okamoto.

I first had a chance to interview her in 1984, when she played in the Portland Ping Championship at Columbia Edgewater Country Club. She still was uncomfortable with the English language at that point, but she willingly responded to questions with an interpreter available to clear up misunderstandings.

She told me a little about her softball career that had gained her fame and adulation in her homeland. She was a left-handed pitcher who led her club team to a national title. Then, at twenty-two, she had an urge to move on and try golf. Her athleticism was such that it took her just two years to become good enough to turn pro. By 1984, when she was thirty-three, she had blossomed into a star in the United States. Of course, that just added to her immense popularity in Japan.

Although intrigued by the challenge of golf, Okamoto admitted that she was naïve and uninformed about the sport when she first took it up. For instance, even though she was a natural lefty, she began playing with right-handed clubs.

"Not know that they make left-handed clubs when I start," she said in her broken English. "Thought right-handed clubs only kind made."

About the time she turned pro, she finally learned that left-handed clubs were available. "Too late to change by that time," she said. "I had hit too many balls [the other way] by then."

She told me, though, that she did try out a left-handed driver one day on a practice range. "I missed ball three straight times. Not have feel."

Okamoto, followed by several Japanese journalists, contended that week in Portland, eventually tying for third place behind winner Amy Alcott. Then, in 1986, she won at Columbia Edgewater by six shots, her score of nine-under-par 207 a tournament record at the time. She followed with four tour wins in 1987, led the money list with $466,034 in earnings and was named LPGA Tour player of the year.

I frequently was reminded of that 1984 interview when the versatile Okamoto went on to win seventeen LPGA Tour tournaments and forty-five international events. She was inducted into the World Golf Hall of Fame in 2005. Not bad for a converted softball pitcher.

## Overreact? Not Carner

JoAnne Carner always had a keen sense of humor in her prime years on the LPGA Tour. I gave thanks for that after an incident involving her at the 1983 Portland tour stop, then called the Ping-Cellular One Championship.

Carner, who compiled an outstanding amateur record while growing up in the Seattle area, had hit a good second shot onto the eighteenth green at Columbia Edgewater Country Club, her final hole of the opening round. The ball ended up fifteen feet from the cup. She had to be thinking birdie as she strolled toward the putting surface, grinning and nodding to spectators along the way.

Earlier, a new photographer at the *Oregonian*, a young woman, had been assigned to the tournament and had introduced herself to me, the golf writer, and asked for instructions.

"I don't play golf and I've never shot [photographs] at a golf tournament," she said. "Please help me out."

Patiently, I gave her tips on what to do and what not to do, and she listened intently. I told her not to snap pictures of a nearby player's swing until after the ball was in flight. I told her she would be allowed inside the gallery ropes with her photographer's pass but that she shouldn't go into the middle of fairways. I also told her to avoid positioning herself too close to the players or in their line of sight while taking her photographs.

She nodded that she understood, and I thought we had covered the necessities. She seemed excited to go to work. I gave her a course map and

JoAnne Carner, here as victorious U.S. captain at the 1994 Solheim Cup, had success and some humorous moments in Portland tournaments. *Photo by Rob Griffin.*

a list of tee times. I also requested that she get some pictures of Carner, a two-time champion of the Portland event.

Now back to Carner and that birdie putt on the eighteenth green. I was behind the green and looking for a good vantage point when I heard some commotion among spectators. I looked and got a sick feeling in my stomach.

There was Carner, standing behind her ball with a puzzled look on her face. About ten feet on the other side of the hole and on the green was our photographer. She was crouched down and ready to take a picture of Carner putting directly at her.

Momentarily, Carner just stared at her, disbelieving. Then she grinned and said, “Do you mind if I play through?”

There was laughter from the gallery, and Carner seemed genuinely amused. The photographer, realizing she had done something wrong, quickly retreated. In all of my instructions, it never had occurred to me that I would need to tell her not to go onto a green with the players.

She came to me in distress, obviously embarrassed. I did my best to calm her and told her not to worry, that I would apologize to Carner for both of us after the round. It would have been nice if Carner had made the birdie putt. She didn’t, settling for a par.

After she had turned in her scorecard, I approached Carner and told her I was sorry for what had happened and explained the photographer’s unfamiliarity with the game. She just smiled and said, “Don’t worry about it. I probably would have missed the putt anyway.”

I suddenly had a feeling of relief and a deeper admiration for Carner’s easy-going and understanding personality. Two days later, there was more relief and admiration. Carner won the tournament, one of forty-three victories that earned her a spot in the LPGA Hall of Fame.

## A Quip Just in Time

Nancy Lopez’s popularity among Oregon golf followers already was booming in 1985 when she played in the Portland Ping Championship at Riverside Golf and Country Club. And her devoted fans were on the verge of being in awe of her cool personality. Nothing seemed to rattle her as she commiserated with spectators before, during and after tournament rounds.

A temper? She seemingly didn’t have one.

“I sometimes get upset, but I’m pretty good at keeping it inside and moving on,” she once told me.

But at Riverside, in the tournament’s opening round, Lopez admitted to being furious after she messed up the twelfth hole, a par four with a sharp dogleg to the left. She made a double-bogey to drop from three-under par to one-under. The smile was gone from her usually jovial face, replaced

Nancy Lopez, a four-time Portland golf champion as a pro, almost had a meltdown on her way to one of those wins. *Photo by Rob Griffin.*

by an uncharacteristic scowl. There was nothing unflappable about her as she walked hurriedly toward the thirteenth tee, her stride seemingly a foot longer than usual.

But on the way, she came upon husband Ray Knight, a player for baseball's New York Mets at the time. "You played that hole like I play," a grinning Knight said. Suddenly, Lopez's smile returned. She took a deep breath and exhaled. A budding temper tantrum had been defused.

"I was really mad but then Ray said that and I laughed," Lopez said. "It really changed my disposition. It calmed me down."

A pivotal moment? Perhaps. Anyway, Lopez regrouped impressively and went on to score the second of her four Portland wins as a professional, beating Lori Garbacz in a playoff.

Interestingly, Knight wouldn't have been there to provide his telling quip if Lopez's bad hole had come later in her round. He had to leave for the airport and a flight to Los Angeles, where the Mets were playing the Dodgers that night.

## Pak: Golf's Pied Piper

When Se Ri Pak showed up in Portland for the 1998 Safeway Classic, she was twenty years old and a budding golf star. Earlier in the year, she had won a pair of majors, the McDonald's LPGA Championship and the U.S. Women's Open. But little did any of us realize the impact that the South Korean's success was going to have in her homeland and on the future of the LPGA Tour.

I should have picked up some clues, though, in interviews I had that week at Columbia Edgewater Country Club. In one of them, Pak talked of the influence that her father, Joon Chul, had had on her golf development. Included were times in her early teens that he insisted that she spend nights alone in a cemetery with a tent and a golf club.

"The first time, I was scared," she said. "Then I came to realize that it was a good place to practice. It was so quiet, and I could think about what I was doing."

Steven Sung-Yong Kil, Pak's manager at the time, helped explain the unusual treatment, so out of line by American standards. He said that her attitude and personality were not an accident but a result of her father's regimented program to make her successful at golf. "There is such an educational and cultural difference in Korea," he said.

Kil then said that Pak's father actually didn't send her to the cemetery to practice golf but to learn how to overcome fear. Then he told of how Chul also took his daughter to dog fights to teach her the importance of winning.

"She had to have her own dog in a fight, too," Kil said. "He wanted her to learn desire from seeing how no one cared about the losing dog left behind."

It was a hint of what was to come as many South Korean fathers realized from Pak's example what could be accomplished with a strict training program and a single-minded purpose. When a young girl showed talent at the game, fathers pushed them and supported them to the limit. Golf was put ahead of education in some cases. Some families even moved to the United States so the daughter could attend one of the golf academies.

Through it all, Pak was the idol to these young South Korean girls. She had shown that success on the LPGA Tour was a reachable goal for them.

Foreign players already were doing well on the tour. Sweden's Annika Sorenstam and Mexico's Lorena Ochoa even became dominating in their play. But the rapid rise of South Korean players brought a kind of dominance that was not only startling but also almost overwhelming.

By 2009, there were forty-seven South Koreans with at least partial exemptions on the LPGA Tour. Birdie Kim opened many eyes when she won the U.S. Women's Open in 2005. Then fellow South Koreans topped the tour money list in 2009 (Jiyai Shin), 2010 (Na Yeon Choi) and 2012 (Inbee Park). The LPGA had itself a new era.

The change has been felt with the Safeway Classic, which has had South Korean winners in 2000 (Mi Hyun Kim), 2004 (Hee-Won Han), 2005 (Soo-Yun Kang) and 2009 (M.J. Hur).

Meanwhile, Pak, who tied for tenth in that 1998 Portland tournament, had won twenty-five LPGA Tour titles through 2012, including five major championships. She already had been inducted into both the World Golf Hall of Fame and the LPGA Tour Hall of Fame.

What a climb it was from her breakthrough year in 1998, when she was the lone South Korean playing the tour. I doubt that she had any idea back then of the stampede-like following she was about to create in her homeland.

## The Three-Peat Barrier

When Annika Sorenstam arrived at Pumpkin Ridge Golf Club in 1997, much of the talk was of her bid to become the first player to win three

Annika Sorenstam, hoping for a record third straight U.S. Women's Open golf title at Pumpkin Ridge in 1997, missed the cut. *Photo by Rob Griffin.*

consecutive titles in the U.S. Women's Open. She tried mightily not to make it a too important part of her goal, knowing that the pressure from such thinking would only add to the difficulty.

"I'm not going to put pressure on myself to make history," Sorenstam told me in a pre-tournament interview at the club west of Portland. Then she said something that made me wonder about that comment: "I've been looking forward to this all year. I feel as if I'm ready."

At the time, Sorenstam was one of six players who had won Opens back to back. But none had been able to nail a third one in a row. Among those who had tried for a three-peat and failed was all-time great Mickey Wright. With the help of an LPGA official, I was able to arrange a telephone interview with Wright, who seldom granted them, from her home in Port St. Lucie, Florida.

"She [Sorenstam] needs to avoid the hype as much as possible," said Wright, who won thirteen major championships among eighty-two career victories. "She just needs to play her own game and let things happen."

Wright's bid for a three-peat came in 1960 at Worcester, Massachusetts. "I remember feeling a lot of pressure," she said. "I probably wanted it too badly."

Wright led after thirty-six holes and was tied for the lead with Betsy Rawls after the third round. Then, uncharacteristically, she struggled to a closing eighty-two and finished fifth as Rawls won. "It was the worst experience I ever had in golf," Wright said. "I blew it."

Sorenstam was due for failure, too. A triple-bogey at the ninth hole of Pumpkin Ridge's Witch Hollow course led to an opening-round seventy-seven, and she missed the cut when she could do no better than a seventy-three in the second round. Alison Nicholas eventually claimed the title by one shot over Nancy Lopez.

Later, in 2002, Karrie Webb became the seventh player to fail in her quest of the elusive Open three-peat. As the years pass, the mental barrier in seeking a three-peat seems to become ever more difficult.

# 17

# THE VIGIL FOR ERIC ROSS

The room was alive with decorations, Get Well posters and cards, balloons, flowers—the works. But there also was an air of apprehension and sadness around the couple who welcomed me that December evening in 1991 at Portland's Emanuel Hospital and Health Center.

Jim and Pam Ross shook my hand and then Jim turned to a nearby bed and said, "Hey, big guy, we've got a visitor; you're missing all the fun."

Lying there on his back was their comatose son, Eric, oblivious to what was going on around him. Or was he?

After his father announced my arrival, I noticed a twitching in one of Eric's hands. It looked as if he were trying to give a thumbs-up gesture. In his other hand, he clung to a rubber Martian man.

"His younger brother, Aaron, gave him the Martian man," Pam said. Aaron had put the Martian man in Eric's hand and said, "This will heal all that ails you." Pam said that Eric had been holding the doll-like figure by the hour ever since, occasionally squeezing it.

Those were just a couple of the encouraging signs that Eric might be close to coming out of a deep coma that he had been in since suffering a football injury five weeks earlier.

Being a sports journalist for a daily newspaper usually means writing, so to speak, about fun and games. It's light stuff for the most part. This was something else involving sports, but much more significant, much more heart-wrenching.

After the death of their son Eric from a football injury, Jim (left) and Pam Ross are introduced at a Pacific game by athletic director Ken Schumann. *Courtesy of Pacific Athletics Media Relations.*

The Rosses, of course, had no idea what was coming when they attended that football game in Forest Grove, Oregon, between Pacific University and Western Washington University (WWU). Eric, a five-foot-nine, 205-pound running back for Pacific, banged into the WWU line on a seemingly routine play when a chest-high tackle flipped him onto his back, his helmeted head banging into the turf.

Play was stopped, but Eric, a twenty-one-year-old senior, was down only momentarily before getting up and staggering to the sideline under his own power. Then, suddenly, he collapsed, and his eyes rolled back in his head. An alert team trainer, Linda McIntosh, recognized a serious concussion and immediately called for a Life Flight helicopter. Within minutes, Eric was being flown to a hospital.

He had bleeding on the brain and swelling. There were surgeries to relieve the pressure.

Thus began the vigil of Jim and Pam Ross, remarkable parents who did all in their power to help their son recover, to force positive thoughts into a brain that obviously was scrambled. They wanted him back, and they wanted to be sure that he knew it.

While I was there that night, Pam stepped forward at one point and grasped one of her son's hands, gently stroked his arm and said, "How's it going, Eric? You know how much we love you." Suddenly, his lips moved, although his eyes remained closed.

Reactions such as this one gave the Rosses constant encouragement. They told me about some other experiences that had kept them hopeful that they could have their son home for Christmas and for his twenty-second birthday on December 26.

Such as the day that Eric opened his eyes and smiled when he saw a photograph of a scantily attired woman that one of his friends had placed on the ceiling above his bed.

"Biggest smile we've gotten out of him yet," Jim said.

Such as the day after his father had told him, "Son, you have to start working your tongue." Jim came into the room and asked, "Eric, have you been working your tongue?" His son responded by sticking out his tongue four times—not far out but far enough for his father to see.

Such as several occasions when Eric gave his parents the thumbs-up sign, a gesture that he always gave them from the football field on game days.

There are those who would say that imagination was involved—that the Rosses simply were reading something into reflex twitches of Eric's body. Well, it wasn't my imagination when I saw that thumbs-up sign as I was introduced. It wasn't my imagination when I saw him clinging to that Martian doll. It wasn't my imagination when I saw his lips move.

The Rosses often read to Eric, and they made sure that his favorite music was his constant companion. Day after day, one of the Rosses, or both, was with Eric from the time that visiting hours began until they ended.

When Jim would come to visit Eric in the late afternoon after work, he would bring along that day's issue of the *Oregonian*. He would turn to the sports section and read to his son.

"He seems to really like that," Jim said. "I read the headlines and then some of the stories, and he opens his eyes and he tracks me with them."

It would be great to write that all this attention eventually paid off. That wasn't the case. After three months in Seattle for stimulation treatments, there were infections, several more surgeries and then two years in a Forest Grove care center before Eric died in 1994, not long after his twenty-fourth birthday. Doctors had warned the Rosses that Eric's death was imminent.

"But we were right there with him day after day until the end," Jim said. "Finally, his body rejected a feeding tube, and he was gone. Pam was convinced that the rejection of that tube was Eric's way of saying that he had had enough."

Thanks to son Aaron's research and suggestion, a cemetery site already had been selected, appropriately one with a view of a nearby school's athletic field.

In the fall of 2010, Pacific University, which had dropped its football program shortly after Eric was injured, revived it. Jim and Pam Ross were invited to attend the school's first home game of the new era, and Pam wore Eric's football jacket with his number, thirty-one, on it. They were introduced and honored at halftime.

Despite Eric's untimely death, the Rosses didn't lose their interest in football, even though they were painfully aware of its brutal nature. After moving from Hillsboro to Bend in Central Oregon, they became avid fans of University of Oregon football and shared season tickets with friends. Jim admitted that they often cringed when a player would go down with an injury, and they would be reminded of Eric.

Then came more tragedy for the Ross family when Pam died of breast cancer in May of 2011.

"She battled it as hard as she could," said Jim, who had moved to a job as business manager of the Deschutes County Sheriff's Office in Bend. "She just couldn't beat it. So now she is buried right next to Eric."

Finally, Jim said that he wasn't sure how much longer he would continue to regularly attend college football games. "Going to the games was something Pam and I enjoyed so much doing together," he said. "It just isn't the same without her."

18

# And That's Entertainment!

It began innocently enough with Dale Thomas, the Oregon State University wrestling coach, giving a preview of his latest team at a 1974 meeting of the Oregon Sportswriters and Sportscasters Association. It was a yawner of a meeting until Thomas decided to liven things up.

Suddenly, his audience at Portland's Multnomah Athletic Club snapped to attention when he unleashed a venomous attack on pro wrestling. He described it as a "complete hoax" on a national scale and "not a legitimate competition." He also said that pro wrestlers "don't even know how to wrestle."

Coming from a person of Thomas's stature as one of the top college wrestling coaches in the country, the blustering stand had sharp teeth. I thought it merited newspaper play and, with an editor's approval, gave it that in the *Oregonian*. A snowball-like reaction came next as some avid pro wrestling followers angrily reacted to the coach's comments.

Nick Sckavone of Portland, president of the National Wrestling Association, pooh-poohed Thomas for his remarks. "The fans are the best judges of what this is all about," he told me. "Between thirty-five and forty million people watch pro wrestling each year."

But considering his lack of an outright denial and reading between the lines, I sensed that even Sckavone recognized that Thomas had a point in branding pro wrestling as entertainment rather than a sporting competition.

Anyway, I did a follow-up story, talking to three pro wrestlers who agreed to answer my questions. One was Bob Pettitt, who also had spent time as a

*Line drawing by Nan Hammerschmidt.*

wrestling promoter before becoming an evangelist and moving to Portland. The other two were retired Oregon wrestlers who had appeared on many cards in Portland and other Pacific Northwest cities. To avoid uncomfortable reactions from the pro wrestling community, the latter two requested that I not reveal their identities. So I gave them the fictitious names of Terrible Tim and Mr. Bighorn.

The three expressed a desire to, as Pettitt said, "put the public straight." All said that Thomas, the national college coach of the year in 1961 and 1970 and later an inductee into the National Wrestling Hall of Fame, had made legitimate points. They agreed, based on their experiences, that pro wrestling was no more a competition than a Broadway play was an enactment of real life.

As for the skills of most pro wrestlers, Terrible Tim said, "Most of them can't wrestle their way out of a wet paper bag." Mr. Bighorn added, "There are some pros who are outstanding athletes, such as Luther Lindsey, Lou Thesz and Pat O'Connor. But eight out of ten pros never even have belonged to an amateur club. They simply went to a pro wrestler and had the pro teach them the business."

As for the outcome of matches, Mr. Bighorn said, "The pro wrestler is told what to do and where to go. He is told whether to win or to lose, and if he doesn't go along, he'll get sent down the road."

Pettitt, twenty-seven at the time, turned to evangelism after spending seven years in the pro wrestling game in the South. He wrestled under several different names, the best known being the Masked Marvel. He willingly described how a match's outcome is arranged.

"First, the promoter tells the wrestlers who is to be the winner and makes any other requests that he might have in the way of action in the ring," he said. "Then the two wrestlers get together and talk out how they will go about bringing the desired result to reality."

Always, Terrible Tim said, the promoter pulls the strings. "The promoter is God," he said. "If he wants blood, the wrestlers give it to him."

Asked how that worked, Mr. Bighorn said, "If you see blood on a wrestler's face, look to see if one of the wrestlers has tape on the end of a finger. A small piece of razor blade is carried under the tape and is used by the wrestler to nick the opponent or himself."

Grudge matches are contrived, too, my three informants proclaimed.

"Hell, the guys in the grudge matches often travel to the sites of their matches together," Mr. Bighorn said. "I did it myself many times. One guy drops the other one off at one restaurant and then goes and eats at another restaurant. That way, they arrive at the arena separately. Then, after the match, they wait until everyone is gone so that they can leave together."

Pettitt even recalled a hilarious situation in the South when he and four other wrestlers—all weighing more than two hundred pounds—took a six-hundred-mile roundtrip for matches in Pettitt's small car. "We had five suitcases, too," he said.

Then the three provided some of the wrestler's jargon, much of it amusingly appropriate.

Dale Thomas, successful Oregon State wrestling coach, started a minor tempest when he attacked pro wrestling at a luncheon. *Courtesy of OSU Athletics Media Relations.*

Start with the fan. He is called the "mark." A bad guy is a "heel," and a good guy is a "baby face."

When a wrestler does a "job," it means that he loses a match. Thus, a "job merchant" is a wrestler who loses frequently.

A "potato punch" is when one wrestler hits an opponent too hard by mistake. "One potato usually is assumed to be an accident," Pettitt said. "But two potatoes in one match will prompt the other wrestler to retaliate."

When a wrestler is said to be "selling," it means that he is making a hold look good. A "crush job" is when a wrestler is sent into the ring with the assignment of making the opponent look good.

A "shooter" is the term for a fellow who is a legitimate athlete. "There usually is one of them in each area," Mr. Bighorn said. "He rules the roost. If one of the guys gets out of line, he is liable to be put in the ring with the shooter."

Finally, the three talked about the expression "Kay Fabian," used by wrestlers as a signal to clam up. For example, a promoter and two wrestlers are in the locker room discussing how a match is to go, and an outsider, not in the know, walks in. One of the three says "Kay Fabian," and talk about the upcoming match ceases.

Once my second story was out, I got an unusual amount of mail and an angry call from Don Owen, who promoted matches in Portland and other Oregon cities for more than thirty-five years. I put the mail in stacks, which had about equal depth.

One stack praised the story as being "great," an "article with insight," an "excellent discussion." The other stack branded the article as "drivel" and described the writer, among other things, as "stupid" and "ignorant" and "one who doesn't know of which he is writing."

The strong reactions prompted me to do a wrap-up column. Included in it were these samplings of the mail that reached my desk:

"I read with amusement your excellent discussion of pro wrestling. This situation has been known to many of us for a long time."—R.C. Rowe.

"…A little boy getting even…an insult to the intelligence of thousands of wrestling fans."—John and Merie Walker.

"It did my heart good to hear what Thomas said. The pro wrestling game, just like the movies, has to have a hero, a villain and a loverboy…[Some] pros do know how to wrestle, but they are not paid to wrestle. They are paid to put on a show."—Cliff Willison.

"I'll tell you what, bring your best amateur…and if Dutch Savage doesn't bend him into pretzels, I'll accept what you say."—Cliff Gerrett.

"I agree totally…on this issue. Let's call professional wrestling what it is, questionable entertainment, and not what it isn't, competitive."—Steve Woods.

"People in pro wrestling work hard to make a living. This is a slur on their occupation."—Dakota Smith.

Even some other former pros responded. One wrote that my articles were "a conspiracy to ruin the good name of wrestling." But another said, "Dale Thomas's reference to pro wrestling being a farce is true and to the point."

Finally, I clarified my position—that my only motive was to put pro wrestling into its true perspective. It was not to destroy pro wrestling as many seemed to feel was the goal. Nowhere did I question its entertainment value.

"If it be your entertainment bag, more power to you," I wrote. "After all, Santa Claus is suspect, too, but nobody is saying that he is not an all right guy."

My feelings are the same today as pro wrestling has moved on to a bigger stage with nationally televised matches that helped make pay-per-view TV a success. It also has become more acceptable among wrestling followers to admit that the outcomes of at least most matches are predetermined.

Thomas, whose Oregon State teams won or tied for twenty-two conference championships, retired in 1990 and was eighty-one when he died in 2004.

Owen, who was ninety when he died in 2002, promoted *Portland Wrestling* on Portland station KPTV from 1952 to 1991 before retiring. He was recognized by the wrestlers as a straight arrow in regards to his payments as promised, a significant contrast with some promoters of the era.

In a sequel, it was more than a month after my articles and column appeared when I answered an office phone and Owen was on the line to give information for an advance story on one of his wrestling cards. I expected a tirade when he learned that he was talking to me. Instead, he was pleasant, a far cry from the angry fellow who had called me earlier. I soon figured out why.

"What you wrote didn't hurt me a bit," he said, laughing. "I have had near sellout crowds ever since that stuff was in the paper. One night, I even ran out of popcorn."

Sometimes, success is measured in strange ways.

# 19

# The Fantasy Title Bout

It was a meaningless conversation, really, but there we were arguing about who would win a fantasy boxing match. It was 1967, and I was in the middle of the discussion with two part-timers in the *Oregonian* sports department.

"I think [Jack] Dempsey would have knocked him out, no question," one of the part-timers said.

"Don't be so sure," I responded. "Don't forget that [Rocky] Marciano had forty-nine fights and won them all."

We were talking about the "championship match" of a computer boxing tournament that had been going for several weeks via radio, the creation of promoter Murray Woroner. The idea was to determine the greatest heavyweight champion of all time by staging a series of mythical bouts with sixteen boxers in the field to start.

The participants were determined through a survey of 250 supposed experts who also were asked to give their evaluations of each of the boxer's strengths, weaknesses, styles and habits. This information then was fed into an NCR 315 computer, then considered a technological wonder, along with each boxer's statistics.

Each week, with Woroner and sportscaster Guy LeBow handling the commentary, another bout was broadcast over a worldwide network. It was a promotion deciding nothing, but it was impossible to resist listening. Mythical or not, curiosity as to the outcomes got the best of many of us.

Anyway, now it was time for the title bout: Dempsey against Marciano. In the semifinals, Dempsey had decisioned Joe Louis, while Marciano had knocked out Jim Jeffries in the fourteenth round.

"I wonder what those two guys think about this," one of the part-timers said.

Suddenly, I had an idea. I said I was going to try and call the two former boxing greats for comments.

The response? "There's no way you'll be able to reach them."

The challenge was irresistible. I offered them a small wager that I could do it, and both jumped at it.

In those days, we had to make long-distance calls through some very efficient *Oregonian* operators. I talked to one and explained what I wanted to do. I told her to try to get Dempsey at his New York restaurant and to see if she could locate Marciano in Brockton, Massachusetts, which was his home when he was fighting.

About ten minutes later, she called back and said she had Dempsey on the line. I talked to him for about fifteen minutes. Another twenty minutes went by and she called me again. "I finally found Mr. Marciano," she said. "He now lives in Fort Lauderdale, Florida. I have him on the line." I interviewed him for about another fifteen minutes, then hung up and gloated over my accomplishment.

I then went to work on a story. I thought that some of their comments made for terrific reading.

Marciano: "When this thing started, I never dreamed I would make it to the final. Many friends have told me that I could have held my own with the greats. I guess I never quite believed them."

Dempsey: "I haven't had a chance to listen to any of the fights so far but I will certainly listen to this one. My wife sure is shook up about it. She went crazy over my fight with Louis. I was away. When I got home, she was shaking all over and couldn't sleep."

Marciano: "This almost is a dream come true for me. As I grew up, Dempsey was my idol. To me, he was the greatest, and he sort of became bigger than life in my mind. Even now, I have trouble thinking of myself alongside him."

Dempsey: "I wasn't surprised that Cassius Clay [later to become Muhammad Ali] lost to Jim Jeffries in this tournament. But if Jeffries hadn't beaten him, there is no question in my mind that Marciano would have knocked him out."

Marciano: "I would have had some things going for me against Dempsey. For instance, Jack didn't fight too well in close, and I was at my best in close.

Conditioning was one of my strong points, and I was better than Dempsey in that regard. The longer the fight goes, the better my chances."

Dempsey: "I probably never fought anyone quite as dangerous as Rocky. He was a good, tough fighter and very fast for his size. He was a fine puncher, and he wasn't as bad a boxer as some say. I would have had to take him out. If I hadn't, he would have taken me out."

Marciano also talked about having "about fifty" friends and relatives coming to his home to listen to the match, although he and Dempsey would be in a studio in Los Angeles close to the booth where Woroner and LeBow would do their broadcast. To ensure that the result wouldn't be leaked, Woroner and LeBow didn't even know the outcome until they were handed sheets showing the computer's round-by-round results by sound engineer Frank Linale.

The winner? Marciano by a knockout at 2:28 of the thirteenth round. Dempsey was knocked down six times but still managed to win four rounds, with four rounds judged even on the computer's scorecard.

Marciano was awarded a gold and diamond championship belt valued at $10,000, a tidy sum in those days. I couldn't help but think of what a great party there must have been at his home in Florida.

As for my part-timer friends and our bets, I told them to keep their money, that the disbelieving looks on their faces as I completed those calls was payoff enough for me.

20

# Memorable Moments

The heckling began several minutes before the opening tipoff at the University of Oregon's McArthur Court, some of it loud and disgustingly personal. "The guy's a geek," one young fellow said. One of his friends piped in with: "No way is he the best basketball player in the state." Another said, "Bob Altenhofen will eat him alive."

A high school senior at the time, I started to stand up and say something to the hecklers a few rows behind us, but my father, Paul Robinson, grabbed my arm and told me to cool it. He reminded me that I was a sportswriter for a weekly newspaper (the *Independence Enterprise*) and that I was supposed to be objective.

"This has nothing to do with me being objective," I told him. "I'm not in the press section, and I'm not covering this game, so I don't have to sit here and ignore that nonsense." But I did ignore it for the time being.

The venom was aimed at Lincoln High School's Wade "Swede" Halbrook, who, at seven feet, three inches, towered over teammates and opponents alike. He and the other Cardinals were about to take on top-ranked Central Catholic and its star, Altenhofen, in the 1952 Oregon big-school championship game.

The chirping from above us continued, even as Halbrook began to single-handedly destroy the Rams. Finally, as the Lincoln lead mounted, I no longer could contain myself. I stood and shouted at the three rowdies, "Hey, guys, look at the scoreboard. As long as the purpose of this game is to put the ball in the basket, Halbrook is by far the best player on the court."

I sat back down, and they laughed at me. But they toned it down after that, and by the game's final buzzer, they had long ago departed.

It was a historic night as Lincoln, coached by Jim Partlow, crushed Central Catholic 66–44. Halbrook, who had Splendid Spire among his nicknames, scored a state tournament record fifty-one points, sinking twenty-four of thirty-six field-goal attempts, most from within a foot or two of the basket. It was halftime before any of his teammates even took a shot as they devotedly followed Partlow's instructions to feed the big fellow.

Halbrook, who went on to play basketball at Oregon State and in the NBA for the Syracuse Nationals, averaged 38.3 points in his senior season at Lincoln with a single game high of seventy-one in a game against Roosevelt of Portland.

When the one-sided title game was over, I offered a less than sincere apology to my father for making a scene. He grinned and said, "Thankfully, you didn't get us into a fight."

## Switching to Olympics Gold

When Otis Davis of the University of Oregon claimed two gold medals at the Rome Olympics in 1960, much was made of him initially being recruited to Oregon to play basketball. He switched to track and field in 1958 after getting limited playing time in basketball.

Later in 1960, while I was sports editor of the *Capital Journal* in Salem, I got an interesting slant on how the switch came

Otis Davis practices starts shortly after switching from basketball to track and field at the University of Oregon. *Courtesy of UO Athletics Media Relations.*

about. It was provided by former UO football player Will Reeve, who at the time was an assistant football coach at South Salem High School. He described to me how he and Davis had worked together on campus jobs at the school's Museum of Art.

"There was a janitor there who kidded around with us a lot, and we did some funny things in our spare moments," Reeve said. "Sometimes, the janitor would hold out a broom handle, and Otis would jump over it. He seemed to go over it so easily that the janitor suggested that he go out for the track team as a high jumper."

Reeve went on to explain that Davis scoffed at the idea at first but that the janitor persisted, hounding him to turn out.

"Finally, one day, Otis decided to give it a try and reported to coach [Bill] Bowerman," Reeve said. "Really, he was recruited to the track team by that janitor. I know that is how it happened because I was there."

It didn't take long for Bowerman to spot Davis's speed and switch him from the high jump to sprinting. As the saying goes, the rest is history. Davis became a major star in Rome, winning the 400 meters in a then Olympic record of 44.9 seconds and anchoring the victorious U.S. 4x400 relay team.

## One That Got Away

Slats Gill was friendly but somber on that spring day in 1964. The Oregon State basketball coach sat in his office in Gill Coliseum, and it was easy to see that he longed to be more a part of the hubbub that was going on elsewhere in the building named after him. His school was preparing to play host to the NCAA West Regional.

For weeks, it had been assumed that the Beavers would be in the field and that Gill, in his final season of coaching, would lead them there. Four days earlier, he was supposed to get his 600th college coaching victory in a sub-regional game against Seattle University at the University of Oregon's McArthur Court. Instead, Seattle scored the game's final twelve points for an improbable 61–57 upset win.

The man who had done so much for basketball and for his school admitted that he was hurting big time. This was anything but the way he anticipated going out. Recollections of the many fine teams he had coached were little consolation to him at this moment.

Slats Gill (center), here with Lew Beck (left) and Red Rocha from the 1946–47 Oregon State team, had his coaching career end sadly. *Courtesy of OSU Athletics Media Relations.*

"I keep replaying the game in my mind and wondering if there was something I could have done differently," Gill said. "I've looked at the films, and I can't find anything that we did wrong in the way of strategy. All the breaks just seemed to go against us at the end."

That Beavers team, led by seven-foot center Mel Counts and the smooth guard tandem of Jim Jarvis and Frank Peters, finished with a 25-4 record but simply came up painfully depth-shy when Jarvis and Peters both fouled out late in the Seattle game. Without them, the Beavers were like a rudderless ship in a storm.

"I still find it hard to believe that we could have blown that lead," said Gill, whose thirty-six year record was 599–392. "In all my coaching career, I never had a seemingly sure win get away as that one did."

As I left Gill's office that day, I felt bad for him, and I couldn't help but reflect on an experience I had with him in 1962 when I was assigned to cover his team's two-game road series against Washington State for the *Oregonian*. It gave me a keen insight into the moral fiber of the man.

Gill invited me to attend the Beavers' practice and then a team dinner the day before the first game of the series. As dinner was concluding at the team's hotel in Pullman, Washington, I overheard Gill say to assistant coach Paul Valenti, "Paul, I would like you to handle the team meeting tonight. Bob wants me to go to a movie with him." That was news to me, but I went along with the ruse.

Thus it was that Gill and I walked about five blocks to an out-of-the-way theater to see the movie *Gypsy*, starring Rosalind Russell and Natalie Wood. The movie was considered a little risqué at the time, and Gill admitted that he was reluctant to have his assistants or the players know that he was attending it.

I told him that I thought he was being overly cautious, but as we left the theater, I assured him that I wouldn't mention where we had gone to anyone in the traveling party. "Thanks, I appreciate that," he said.

## Meeting the Blond Kid

I was relaxing in the media room at Eugene Country Club on that overcast but warm July day in 1964 when a U.S. Golf Association official approached. He said, "There's a blond kid from San Francisco out there shooting up a storm."

It was the second day of qualifying for the U.S. Junior Amateur, and I was looking for a story angle. This sounded like a possibility. Out to the course I went, and that's when I got my first look at Johnny Miller, who would go on to fame on the PGA Tour and, later, as a television golf analyst.

Miller, seventeen at the time, shot a sixty-eight that day, four under par, and called it "the best round of my life." It helped earn him the qualifying medal. Then he went on to win the championship, edging Enrique Sterling of Mexico City two and one in the match play final.

Looking back, I recall how shy Miller was in a post-round interview after his second qualifying round. A pinkness crept into his cheeks, and he frequently looked at the ground while replying to my questions.

Some of the players had complained about the tightness of Eugene CC's fairways, but not Miller. "I play golf in San Francisco at the Olympic Club," he said. "It is a tough course, and that has helped me here. I'm used to long holes and lots of trees."

Miller perhaps came the closest to defeat that week in the first round against Louis Anderson of Alexandria, Virginia. He was one down through eleven holes and faced a fifteen-foot par putt at the twelfth hole to keep from falling two down. As he prepared to putt, I heard him say to his caddie, "I've got to make this putt or it's just about all over."

Then he sank the putt and surged to a three-and-two victory. As the week ran its course, it wasn't difficult for me to tell that I was watching a player about to have a major impact in the golf world.

## A Flip on the Flop

When Dick Fosbury won the high jump gold medal at the 1968 Olympics in Mexico City, few people realized what a difficult time he had convincing Berny Wagner, his college coach at Oregon State, that his personally developed flop style was worth pursuing.

In an interview a few years later, Wagner admitted that he had been an extremely tough sell. Like so many people, he considered Fosbury's style no more than a gimmick that soon would be forgotten.

Dick Fosbury clears a high jump bar with his flop style that won over his college coach and changed the event worldwide. *Courtesy of OSU Athletics Media Relations.*

"I first saw Dick jump at an all-comers meet in Gresham [Oregon]," Wagner said. "I was impressed with the heights he was jumping, but I thought to myself, 'What a screwy innovation.' I recruited him because I was sure that he could go higher [than his high school best of six feet, five and a half inches] when we got him jumping the conventional way."

Wagner showed patience and flexibility, allowing Fosbury to use the flop, going over the bar back first, in meets as a freshman. But he insisted that he keep working on the straddle style, going over the bar with the face down, in practice.

Then came a defining moment in Fosbury's first meet as a sophomore. Using the flop, he cleared six feet, ten inches with seeming ease. Wagner said he immediately did a flip on the flop. Suddenly, he became one of the strongest and most significant advocates of Fosbury's method.

"He made me a believer that day," Wagner said. "I realized that others could do the flop, too, and we went to work hard on it."

Such is the way Fosbury began to revolutionize the high jump. After he claimed the 1968 gold medal with an Olympic Games record of seven feet, four and one-fourth inches, his method rapidly became the most popular worldwide, and high jump records began to tumble.

## Dealing with Pre

Watching Steve Prefontaine run a distance race often was like watching an actor give an Academy Award performance. The little guy with hard-to-believe stamina simply was amazing, and so were Pre's People, the fanatic followers he drew at the University of Oregon's Hayward Field.

But for the media, he wasn't always easy to deal with. Although I was involved in track and field coverage only occasionally at the time, I had been annoyed a couple of times when Prefontaine had shown impatience with my post-race questioning. So at an Oregon dual meet in 1972, three years before he died tragically in a car accident, I was determined to have a comeback if he played smart aleck with me.

As it turned out, it was pouring rain when Prefontaine ran in a two-mile race. And he ran a remarkable time considering the conditions. He won easily and then, with his customary entertainment flair, did a victory lap, smiling and waving to the applauding fans. Finally, I caught up with him and got that impatient look that he sometimes displayed when a member of the media approached.

I started by asking him how much better he thought his time might have been if the weather hadn't been so miserable. He frowned and said, "You ask questions like the Los Angeles writers."

For once, I thought of a comeback on the spot. I said, "That makes us even because you answer questions like the Los Angeles runners."

There was a moment of silence, and Prefontaine gave me a frosty stare. Then he broke into a grin. "Good one," he said.

We talked for about ten minutes after that, and I never again had a significant problem when I approached him for an interview.

## The Race for the Aged

While I was covering the Portland Trail Blazers on their run to the 1977 NBA championship, radio broadcaster Bill Schonely and I often jogged together on road trips while the team practiced. Sometimes we were outdoors, sometimes on the concourse of an arena. It became a joking debate among the players about which one of us was the fastest. "One of you is slow and the other slower," one wisecracking player said.

Bill Schonely, longtime radio voice of the Portland Trail Blazers, lost a footrace and got a pie in the face in 1977. *Portland Trail Blazers archive photo.*

That's all the incentive that team trainer Ron Culp, a master at practical jokes, needed to orchestrate a race between us. I was having breakfast in a hotel coffee shop one day on the team's last regular-season road trip when Culp approached. "Schonely says he can beat you running," he said. I laughed and replied, "That's bull. He can't."

Then, I found out later, Culp had gone to Schonely and said, "Robbie says you don't have enough guts to race him."

The next thing I know, Culp announces to the Blazers coaches and players that the two of us would have a match race at the first team practice after the road trip, the winner getting to put a pie in the face of the loser. Schonely was forty-eight at the time, and I was forty-three. I still question our sanity for agreeing to participate.

Anyway, I didn't think Schonely would show up at the practice, but he did, and we donned running shoes and clothes for the race in Portland's Memorial Coliseum. Players made bets on the sideline. Culp even had arranged for two TV stations to film the race. The course was end line to end line and back with coach Jack Ramsay as the starter and assistant Jack McKinney at the other end to make sure we touched the line before making the return trip.

I was confident I would win, but Schonely surprised me with his effort. I won by less than a foot. With the cameras rolling, I splashed a lemon meringue pie in his face, and laughter echoed. Then, with order seemingly restored, I went to work interviewing backup center Robin Jones for a story.

A tap on the shoulder interrupted me. It was guard Lionel Hollins asking if he could look at my glasses. Earlier, I had told him how pleased I was with my new photo-gray lenses. I handed him the glasses—a terrible mistake—and Schonely suddenly appeared and plastered me with a pie. The intentions of the deceitful Culp were clear. He had arranged to have two pies on hand.

There was an interesting sequel. The Blazers, who had lost four of five games on their last trip, suddenly began playing better and won six in a row to finish the regular season. Naturally, Schonely and I claimed that our race had provided the players with a mental boost that aided their turnaround.

## A Miracle Comeback

The Portland Trail Blazers, the defending NBA champions, had been on a torrid run. They had won thirty-six consecutive games in their home Memorial Coliseum over two seasons when the Chicago Bulls visited on January 3, 1978. The Bulls played extremely well and seemingly had the Blazers on the ropes with a 90–86 lead and the final seconds ticking away.

From my seat on press row, I noticed several fans making early exits, something that usually only happened when Portland was blowing out an opponent. As it turned out, they missed something special. With defeat imminent, the Blazers pulled off an improbable comeback, scoring six points in eight seconds to win 92–90 and make it thirty-seven in a row. And the three-point shot wasn't yet a part of basketball's rules.

Lionel Hollins had two of the field goals when the Trail Blazers made a miracle rally in 1978. *Portland Trail Blazers archive photo.*

The rally began when Maurice Lucas worked free in the key and sank a jumper with ten seconds left to make it 90–88. Then, after a Chicago timeout, Lionel Hollins stole the inbounds pass and scored on a layup with seven seconds remaining to tie the game at 90–90. Chicago called another timeout before Bob Gross deflected Norm Van Lier's inbounds pass. Dave Twardzik retrieved the ball and passed it to a streaking Hollins for the game-winning layup with two seconds left.

The next day, I had some fun by calling a couple of Portland taxi companies and arranging to talk to drivers who had picked up customers leaving the Coliseum early the night before. One cabbie, who was listening to the game on the radio, picked up his customer just as the rally was ending.

"The guy heard what had happened and was really upset with himself for missing the finish," he said. "I hadn't heard so many obscenities in a long time."

## Catching the Heat

One of the endearing characteristics of Portland golf pro Peter Jacobsen's personality is that he is the same person on or off the golf course. Friend P.J. Carlesimo, a longtime National Basketball Association coach, put it this way in a 1996 interview: "You see how much fun he is on the golf course, but I

Peter Jacobsen heads a golf laugh fest in 1989. *From left to right*: Mark Calcavecchia, Curtis Strange, Andy Bean, Jacobsen, Bob Tway and Arnold Palmer. *Photo by Tom Treick.*

can't say enough about how much fun he is away from the course. There is no one I would rather spend time with than him."

Part of Jacobsen's makeup revolves around his habit of not taking himself too seriously. One-liners are a way of life with him. The trait helped make him a popular host of the Fred Meyer Challenge golf tournament, a Portland event that ran from 1986 to 2002, lured many of the game's top players and drew large crowds. It often turned into a laugh fest.

Occasionally, though, Jacobsen's easy-going way draws ire from those who lack a sense of humor. Such was the case in 1992, when Jacobsen's beloved Portland Trail Blazers were playing the Chicago Bulls in the NBA Finals and he was interviewed on a national telecast. At the time, Bulls star Michael Jordan had made comments that he was considering a try at the PGA Tour after his basketball-playing days.

Jacobsen was asked what he thought of Jordan's chances of having a tour career. He replied, "I'll be playing center for the Chicago Bulls before Michael Jordan plays on the PGA Tour."

A few weeks later, Jacobsen laughed when I asked him what kind of reactions he had gotten to his evaluation of Jordan's golf future. "I took a lot of heat in Chicago over that one," he said.

# Index

# INDEX

# About the Author

*Photo courtesy of Donna Robinson.*

Branding Bob Robinson as a lifelong sportswriter is a stretch, but it's not far from fact. He began covering high school sports in 1946, when he was twelve and in the sixth grade, and his career path seldom wavered after that.

That first writing experience came in Independence, Oregon, where he was recruited for the assignment by Ralph Kletzing, owner and publisher of the weekly *Independence Enterprise*. He continued in that capacity through his two years at Independence High School and then two more years at Central High School, a consolidation of students from Independence and Monmouth. Frequently, he played on teams that he was writing about.

The enjoyment that Robinson got from that start led him to the University of Oregon and his eventual graduation from the UO School of Journalism in 1956. While in college, he got the feel of working for a daily newspaper with part-time employment in the sports department of the *Eugene Register-Guard*, where Dick Strite was the sports editor.

# ABOUT THE AUTHOR

After his graduation, he spent five years at the *Capital Journal* in Salem, Oregon, serving stints as assistant news editor, city editor and sports editor before joining the *Oregonian* sports department staff in the fall of 1961. He remained there for thirty-seven and a half years, turning to freelance writing after his retirement in 1999.

At the *Oregonian*, he was the golf writer for more than thirty years and also had a variety of other assignments. He was the beat writer for the Portland Trail Blazers when they won the NBA championship in 1977, and he also covered college sports at Oregon State, the University of Oregon, Portland State and the University of Portland.

This is Robinson's fourth book, following *Golf in Oregon: Historic Tales from the Fairway* (The History Press, 2012).

Earlier, he wrote two books after the Blazers' title run—*World Champions* (Graphic Arts, 1977) and *Bill Walton: Star of the Blazers* (Scholastic Book Services, 1978). He also wrote chapters for two other books—*Chicken Soup for the Golfer's Soul: The Second Round* (Health Communications, 2002) and *Red Hot and Rollin'* (Nestucca Spit Press, 2007).

Robinson, a Portland resident for more than fifty years, was selected by his peers as Oregon's Sportswriter of the Year in 1977. He also was honored for his contributions to golf with the Peter Jacobsen Award in 1997, the Dale Johnson Media Award in 2003 and the Northwest Golf Media Association's Distinguished Service Award in 2004.